D0907095

Building Strong
Nonprofits

Building Strong Nonprofits

NEW STRATEGIES FOR GROWTH AND SUSTAINABILITY

Edited by

John C. Olberding and Lisa Barnwell Williams

WILEY

John Wiley & Sons, Inc.

Published by John Wiley & Sons, Inc., Hoboken, New Jersey.
Published simultaneously in Canada.

For general information on our other products and services or for technical support, please contact our Customer Care Department within the United States at (800) 762-2974, outside the United States at (317) 572-3993 or fax (317) 572-4002.

Wiley also publishes its books in a variety of electronic formats. Some content that appears in print may not be available in electronic books. For more information about Wiley products, visit our web site at www.wiley.com.

Library of Congress Cataloging-in-Publication Data

Building strong nonprofits : new strategies for growth and sustainability / edited by John C. Olberding and Lisa Barnwell Williams.
    p. cm
Includes bibliographical references and index.
ISBN 978-0-470-58787-4 (cloth)
1. Nonprofit organizations—Management.   2. Nonprofit organizations.
I. Olberding, John C.   II. Williams, Lisa Barnwell
    HD62.6.B85 2010
658.4'012—dc22

                                                          2009050967

Printed in the United States of America

10 9 8 7 6 5 4 3 2 1

*The editors and authors dedicate this volume to Robert L. Thompson,
legendary head of the respected fundraising
consulting firm of Ketchum, Inc.,
and long-time colleague, partner, and member of the
Skystone Ryan Board of Directors.*

Contents

Contents

Contents

Acknowledgments

Many of the individuals who assisted in the development of chapters are thanked therein. In addition, the editors want to acknowledge the contributions of the following:

- Skystone Ryan partners Blanche Gaynor, Elizabeth Knuppel, and Jack Kerber, for editorial assistance.
- Our office team, Pam Wallace and Marcia Butler, for supporting our efforts.
- Skystone Ryan consultant and author Martin Novom, for sharing with us the experience he garnered working with John Wiley & Sons on his 2007 book, *The Fundraising Feasibility Study: It's Not About the Money.*
- Susan McDermott and the John Wiley team, both for providing the opportunity for Skystone Ryan to share our expertise and for their invaluable support in the preparation of this initial volume.

Introduction

Welcome to an exciting new adventure!

All of us at Skystone Ryan Inc. are, at heart, idealists. We want to use our energy and talent to make the world a better place. We find professional satisfaction, and indeed joy, in advocating for the world of nonprofit organizations as they educate and inspire, uplift and heal, convert and care for our fellow man.

We do this quietly every day as we work with nonprofits throughout the country and around the world to energize their advocates and benefactors, to set—and surpass—challenging financial goals, and to discover their greatness.

We also delight in doing this within our profession by serving on the boards of local chapters of the Association of Fundraising Professionals, speaking at workshops and conferences, teaching academic courses on fundraising and nonprofit management, publishing our *Issues in Philanthropy* newsletter, mentoring colleagues, promoting scholarly professional development by awarding the *Skystone Ryan Prize for Research*, and in many other ways.

Now, we are especially honored by the invitation from John Wiley & Sons to share our perspectives and our expertise with you who are our professional colleagues in a new way, through the publication of *Building Strong Nonprofits: New Strategies for Growth and Sustainability*. Once or twice each year we will be writing about the topics that touch each of us as development professionals. Our hope is that we can be a partner with you in your continuing education, in your path to greater success in serving others through philanthropy.

Frankly, our aspiration for this series is high: We want to assist you to become a philanthropist, in the fullest sense of that word. As we view it, a philanthropist is one who cares deeply for others, one who is committed to giving of self to support those cases that serve mankind. We want to help you on that noble career journey by sharing with you new insights, new tools, new ways of thinking, of doing, of leading, and of serving. We want to help you as you live out your own personal commitment to generously give your time, your drive, indeed your professional life to the noble task of promoting the common good. Come along with us on this exciting adventure!

J. Patrick Ryan
Chairman
Skystone Ryan Inc.

SKYSTONE RYAN BELIEVES THAT PHILANTHROPY LIES AT THE HEART OF HUMAN GREATNESS

Founded in 1975, Skystone Ryan Inc. is one of the nation's leading fundraising consulting firms. With offices in cities across the United States and affiliated firms in Canada, Mexico, and around the globe, the firm works with nonprofit organizations of every size, including colleges and universities, professional associations, civic and cultural groups, social service agencies, hospitals, and religious organizations. Much of Skystone Ryan's work focuses on planning and executing capital campaigns, but we also facilitate or provide planned and annual giving programs, prospect research, institutional planning, board development, staff training, executive search, development-related writing and graphic design, and a host of other services. Skystone Ryan draws its strength from a diversity of client experience; a tailored, team approach by senior professionals; an international perspective; and service from fully staffed regional offices.

Building Strong Nonprofits

CHAPTER 1

A New Day for Philanthropy

JOHN C. OLBERDING

"It was *not*," she declared, "October 29, 1929. That was not the Great Depression's most important moment." My grandmother paused dramatically, almost reverentially, as she recalled her most vivid memory of that time.

"It was the day," she declared, "that Roosevelt closed the banks."

"That's when everything changed."

March 6, 1932, was practically a sacred day to Granny, because, as she put it, "We knew, finally, that we would be all right. That things would change—they would *have* to change—and that each one of us could play a small part in that change."

Historians may argue the economic importance, and even the legality of President Franklin Roosevelt's action—his first official proclamation upon taking office. But to hear my grandmother describe it, "The sun's place which was so low on the horizon for the past several years seemed finally that day to be more dawn than dusk."

"Instead of wondering if there would even be a tomorrow, we began to ask ourselves what we would do with today."

One answer to that question over the subsequent years came in the way the country began to adjust the ways in which it supported public charities. A number of landmark developments signaled a real and palpable evolution in philanthropy:

- *The National Society for Crippled Children launched in 1934* its first "Easter Seals" campaign, introducing a national campaign strategy based on the simple concept of buying and affixing stamps to letters to the entire country. The next year, President Franklin Roosevelt announced the creation of the *National Foundation for Infantile Paralysis* and, in 1938, Eddie Canter coined the name *"March of Dimes"* as he urged radio listeners to send their spare change to the White House to be used in the fight against polio. In many ways these initiatives, using what were then modern mail and mass communication techniques, began the national democratization of philanthropy that today we take for granted as the foundation of a charitable society.
- *Through the Revenue Act of 1935,* corporate foundations were codified in U.S. tax law by permitting corporations to deduct charitable contributions up to five percent of taxable income. Together with the emergence of the Community Chest, corporate philanthropy could be seen as a separate and significant force.
- *In 1935, the American Association of Fund-Raising Counsel* was formed—the first organization to recognize the design and effective execution of charitable fundraising efforts and practices as a profession.
- *In 1935, the Winston-Salem Community Foundation* received its first donor-advised funds. Today there are more donor-advised funds in the United States than traditional private foundations.
- *The Ford Foundation was chartered in 1936* by Edsel Ford and two Ford Motor Company executives "to receive and administer funds for scientific, educational and charitable purposes, all for the public welfare." After the death of Edsel and Henry Ford, it became the world's largest foundation and expanded its mission to "promoting peace, freedom, and education throughout the world." Combined with the movement toward the global initiatives of the Kellogg Foundation (also founded in the 1930s), the Ford Foundation led the way toward a new

internationalization of philanthropy that would be spurred by World War II and its aftermath.

- In 1937, John Rockefeller died, leaving an estate worth $1.4 billion and bequests to charity totaling $530 million. To comprehend the magnitude of this estate today, economists estimate that as a measure of share of GDP today, it would be worth $210 billion, or roughly seven times the net assets of the Bill and Melinda Gates Foundation!

It is difficult to imagine the impact of these various events—all happening in the span of just five years—on modern philanthropy. The Great Depression was a catalyst for what today we know as corporate philanthropy, professional fundraising, fundraising by mail and media, donor-advised funds, "mega-gifts," and international fundraising.

It is not too much of a stretch, then, to see parallels in today's philanthropic landscape. Following the worst economic crisis since the Great Depression, we are faced with a new menu of opportunities and challenges stoked by technology and tempered by an awareness of finite resources. How we recognize and respond to those opportunities and challenges is sure to shape the face of philanthropy for decades to come.

The Big Picture

The pages that follow explore how the philanthropic sector might evolve in such specific areas as social media, the global economy, social entrepreneurship, and cause-related marketing. Seen together, though, a number of themes emerge that may provide some insight into the next generation of philanthropy. Philanthropic trends follow greater political and social movements—toward or away from democratization or specialization, for example—and many of the predictions and trends identified in this book are based on our individual and collective judgments as to what course the next generation may take. At the end of the day, these are subjective predictions (I think the shock of the Great Recession has humbled many in the forecasting business!), but we hope they may be useful in planning the important work of the nonprofit community in the years to come.

What Will Be Different

Here, then, are one person's thoughts on what is likely to be quite different—and quite similar—in the philanthropic world in the years to come.

Personal Philanthropy Will Increase Dramatically

In both total contributions and as a percentage of wealth, I believe that we will see a substantial increase in giving over the next decade for the first time since records have been reliably kept. Do I believe that human nature will suddenly change and people will be simply spontaneously more generous? In a word, no. There are several mechanical and social factors, however, that I think will spur greater personal giving.

The first factor related to public benefit organizations is the palpable *shift in funding from public to private sectors*. This is happening both in the United States and, increasingly, worldwide. In short, governments are politically losing the ability to tax. Even the most socialist countries and the most liberal states and localities have found that increasing taxes is practically impossible. Meanwhile, the press of increasing demands caused by a number of factors—population growth, upward mobility, deferred social investments, to name just a few—will be shifted to the philanthropic sector. More and more, governments themselves are getting into the fundraising business. Areas that were once primarily publicly funded, such as libraries, parks, and government-owned hospitals, are now opening or dramatically enhancing fundraising offices. Public funds that are available will increasingly come with private fundraising strings. This hardly means that there is a greater need for funds in the next generation than there were needs in generations (much less centuries) past. It does mean, however, that the sheer volume of solicitations will grow significantly and giving is likely to follow.

Secondly, the next generational transfer of wealth is likely to skew far more to charitable causes than to family. Some of this is based on simple demographics: the affluent of today have fewer family members than those of the past. But many of us who have been working with nonprofit organizations for over a quarter century have also noticed a more fundamental change in the ethos of conspicuous consumption and estate planning encapsulated in the question Jack Nicholson's private eye, J.J. Gittes, asked of John Houston's water-robbing mogul, Cross, in the Depression-set *Chinatown:* "Then why are you doing it? How much better can you eat? What can you buy that you can't already afford?"

The past generation of conspicuous consumption, like the Roarin' Twenties, seems poised to be followed by an era of greater generosity. The very wealthy will be more able and more inclined to make the kind of transformational gifts once relegated to the Fords, Rockefellers, MacArthurs, Gates, and Kelloggs. That will be especially true, I believe, in wealth transference. Certainly, children born into great wealth will continue to enjoy the benefit of family wealth, but there will be fewer such children and the benefits will have limits. In recent years, I have heard several quite affluent individuals offer something like: "My family will be well-enough cared for; they don't need to have everything handed to them." I never used to hear that. Even more gratifying is that I also hear more and more family members agree. I definitely never used to hear *that!*

Beyond greater demands on philanthropy and an emerging culture that might better promote it, I anticipate that the fundraising profession will reach a new level of maturity and competence. Fundraising will be buoyed by better clinical research in the field, more extensive educational offerings than ever before, and greater efficiencies propelled by technological and communication advancements. We have a long way to go in all of those areas, to be sure, but it stands to reason that a larger, more experienced, and vastly better equipped and educated profession will have a catalytic effect on overall giving.

The Nonprofit Sector Will See Both Major Consolidation and Diversification

I believe we will see competing currents that will dramatically alter the landscape of philanthropy over the next generation.

On one hand, the spate of mergers and consolidations begun in the past decade in education and health care is likely to extend to the arts, to associations, and to the environmental and social service organizations. The financial crisis that most charitable organizations experienced over the last years has forced many to openly, honestly, and bravely look at fundamental questions of mission, organization, and "competition." The corporate and foundation communities, in particular, have long encouraged nonprofits to consider consolidation with others with similar missions; those encouragements will increasingly have carrots and sticks accompanying them.

On the other hand, the preference of the next generation of philanthropists is clearly toward a more personal customized approach. The explosion of donor-advised funds is one indication. So is the burgeoning of giving circles and social entrepreneur institutes, clubs, and associations. The Internet makes it possible to craft "boutique" charitable organizations in a customized and immediate way that will provide greatly more diversified and specific choices. No disease will be too rare, no art will be too arcane, no service will be too remote or specific to have its own Web site and related fundraising opportunity.

These cross-currents of propagation and consolidation of nonprofit organizations combined with a more "hands-on" attitude by more and more donors will promote, I imagine, the cottage industry of donor advocacy. As consultants to nonprofit organizations, we are already seeing an interest in such donor-centric assistance.

Larger consolidated organizations will have greater appeal for larger institutional donors, such as corporations and major foundations wishing to form effective strategic partnerships. They will not be as content as in the past to simply publish giving criteria and wait for the mail to arrive with that quarter's proposals. They will be proactive in seeking out—or even creating—those organizations that can best leverage their social and financial investment. They will also welcome objective assistance in finding suitable partners in both the philanthropic and charitable communities.

An example of this approach is one fostered in recent years by several major foundations in forming the Africa Grantmakers Affinity Group. These blue-chip foundations—Carnegie, Ford, Hewlett,

Kresge, MacArthur, Mellon, Rockefeller—recognized in 2004 that the formidable demands on the philanthropic sector of promoting, for example, higher education in Africa would benefit from partnership and consolidation of efforts. In the future, I believe, more such affinity groups will be formed among donors and charities alike with a focus that begins with an opportunity or problem to be solved, and *then* they'll find partners—as opposed to the traditional approach where an individual institution identifies a need and seeks to fulfill that need itself.

Another kind of philanthropic "matchmaking" will develop with individual donors and smaller or "boutique" charities at the other end of this trend line. In these instances, an individual may be interested in say, public education at the high school level using the Montessori Method. Perhaps he or she was inspired by a positive experience with Montessori at the lower levels and had heard of recent but limited positive developments in extending this pedagogy to the secondary level.[1] The traditional approach would have this individual incorporate a new foundation, attempt to find a few like-minded individuals (typically from among friends, family and associates) and begin with a local project in a local school. In the new paradigm, however, such an idea and such an individual need not be so limited. Using Web-based social networks and simple search engines to complement traditional networks, the individual philanthropist or representative can test the waters on a far more global basis. They'll find both fellow funders and already-developing capital or research projects to address the "cause" in a more comprehensive and organic process. It is, to be sure, a model of organizational development with its own pitfalls and tradeoffs, but one that is nonetheless likely to be more and more common in the generation ahead.

The new philanthropic landscape, then, will be particularly dynamic. There will be something like geometric growth in the number of moving parts: size, number, specialization, breadth, culture, location, to name just a few variables. This will certainly lead to the potential for great marketplace confusion as the sheer volume of movement will make for a degree of instability that may be nerve-racking and exciting at the same time for donors and charities alike.

Ironically, the short-term effect of this dynamism may well be that well-established traditional nonprofits such as churches and schools will have an even stronger position. Key older and more affluent constituents will tend to hold fast to the masts of their local congregation or their alma maters amid the greater turbulence.

The Fundraising Profession Will Be Besieged by Critical Personnel Shortages, Scandal, and Counterproductive Regulation

The downside of greater societal reliance on philanthropy worldwide and the increased diversification and consolidation within the field will be acceleration of a troublesome cycle in the profession: a shortage of trained and competent professionals leads to greater likelihood of scandal and corruption, which leads to greater rules and restrictions on fundraising professionals, which leads to greater shortages of qualified professionals. To better understand this cycle, it may be useful to consider the evolution of the profession from the hallowed halls of academia to the frequently unwelcome ring of the telephone at dinnertime.

At the time in 1969 that my father, Greg, made the decision to move from a career in public relations into fundraising, the field was barely and loosely recognized as a profession. Even the national gatherings of what was then the 10-year-old National Society of Fund Raising Executives were held in small hotel ballrooms with attendance measured in the hundreds. He was typical of those who would gather at that time, coming to the profession out of a genuine interest in charitable work (he was a former seminarian and teacher who had worked at the local Community Chest), but with no academic or formal training in the field. There was little pertinent literature (though he did proudly pass on to me his copy of the seminal *Designs for Fundraising*, by Harvard's Harold J. "Sy" Seymour). The primary sources of wisdom, experience or thought were available for those in a campaign and hiring professional counsel or through exchanging ideas with each other. When Dad joined the staff of St. Xavier High School in Cincinnati, fundraising was still only part of his job.

Today, that same Jesuit school has a professional staff of 10, and our professional organization, now called the Association of

Fundraising Professionals, numbers over 20,000 from all around the world. There is a well-stocked library of literature in the field (to which we hope the Skystone Ryan series is a welcome addition), and a number of formal academic programs have been instituted, led by the Center for Philanthropy in Indianapolis. Admirable as is much of this progress, however, it is woefully inadequate to meet the explosion in demand for competent stable ethical professionals.

The fundraising profession still suffers from many of the same dynamics that my father encountered upon entering it 40 years ago: unreasonable and inconsistent expectations, inadequate academic or professional training or standards, and a built-in "glass ceiling" in the nonprofit sector that encourages frequent job changes for the best and brightest. The average work span of a director of development in a given nonprofit organization is estimated at 20 months. By the time those professionals have gone through one calendar year of appeals and events and funding cycles with an organization and are just beginning to be familiar with the mission and to develop personal relationships with donors and volunteers, they leave. Why?

In economic terms that might be employed in the for-profit sector, the supply of capable human resources is simply not keeping up with the demand. There are nearly one million nonprofit organizations in the United States alone and only a small fraction are staffed in their fundraising efforts by professionally trained or adequately experienced staff. That by no means reflects on the dedication, intelligence, or commitment of the organizations or staffers who do not have such experience or staffing; just a simple function of mathematics. To compensate, the for-profit market would say that a great fundraising executive would be given incentive by commensurate monetary compensation, for instance, or by a significant investment in professional development, and that such monetary compensation would be a wise investment. For better and for worse, however, that principle does not apply as much to the culture and sensitivity of charitable organizations. Not every value can be reduced to fiscal terms. It is unseemly to pay the market rate for an organization's fundraising professional when the market rate for that same organization's chief social worker, or educator, or curator is very often so much lower.

So, an understandable but often counterproductive glass ceiling is created; a talented professional who gains experience at one organization realizes his or her market value only by moving to the next stop.

Unfortunately, that is not the only reason for the profession's high turnover. Often, the person or persons hiring and supervising the development professional, or the individuals applying themselves, simply fail to understand the job. "Fundraising" means many different things to many different people, and expectations for a particular position by one or both parties are often either unrealistic or unclear. In the absence of those with experience or training, the natural inclination is to look at "related" professions, with unpredictable results. Someone who is, say, a good volunteer or a good salesperson may make, with decent training or coaching, a great fundraising professional—or a lousy one. The reality is that with no better alternatives, the wrong people are often hired, or the right people are hired but often evaluated incorrectly. Or they simply move on to better positions.

The growing staffing crisis in professional fundraising combines with several other factors touched on earlier—the dramatic and dynamic growth of the nonprofit sector and its blurred boundaries with the government and for-profit sectors—to provide the makings of scandal and corruption. Any time large amounts of money change hands with less than professionally adequate oversight and within increasingly complex organizations, there is the opportunity for mischief. It is a tribute to the sacred position of philanthropy in our collective *ethos*, frankly, that scandals regarding charitable gifts have historically been few and mundane. To be sure, some individual organizations have been severely hurt by incidents of excess, scheming, and occasional abject fraud, but the world of philanthropy as a whole has yet to be rocked by a significant scandal.

I am afraid that will change in the coming years.

I promise to you and the authorities that I have no firsthand knowledge or insight into any particular malfeasance. I certainly hope I am mistaken. But if crimes are based on motive and opportunity, human nature has long provided the motivation to do evil as well as good, and it seems that there will be unprecedented opportunity. If robbers rob banks because "that's where the money is," as more money goes toward charity, the largest of those charities may become targets for the biggest crimes. If such a crime occurs—via Ponzi scheme, extortion, embezzlement or the like—tightened regulations for both charity and donor will inevitably follow.

This will put added pressure on medium-sized organizations particularly to merge or consolidate and on the profession to screen and police its own members. In one sense, of course, such regulations are quite healthy. In the late 1980s, many of us worked with the federal government, Financial Accounting Standards Board, and state Attorneys General to write good model charitable solicitation laws designed to codify legitimate fundraising efforts. In many states, however, those model laws have been superseded by ill-conceived or poorly defined new regulations that tend to add expense and counterproductive new bureaucracy to charities and the professionals who would serve them. A major new scandal will only accelerate this trend.

What Will Not Change

We are focused in this volume primarily upon new opportunities and challenges facing the world of philanthropy in the next generation. It is worth noting, however, some fundamentals of philanthropy that we do not expect to be significantly altered in the foreseeable future.

Personal Relationships Have Dominion

The pioneering Australian fundraising consultant and long-time colleague Michael Downes puts it this way: "*Who asks* is more important than 'What for.'"

For all of the coming dynamics we predict here in the size, volume, character, and practices of nonprofit organizations, fundraising has been and will ever be, at its core, one person asking another person on behalf of someone else. The way I often illustrate this basic precept is by suggesting two scenarios in which you are approached for what, for you, would be a "stretch" gift to a particular organization—the kind of gift you could only make this once.

In the first, you are approached on behalf of an organization to which you have a natural and strong affinity. The attendant materials are thorough and top-notch. The "pitch" is professional and convincing, but delivered by a perfect stranger.

In the second, you are approached by the person you care about most in the world: someone you trust implicitly. That person tells you that they urgently need your help with something that is the most important thing they have ever done. You don't know anything else. There are no materials. There is no pitch.

To which solicitation are you more likely to respond with the requested gift?

When I ask this question in presentations, the response is overwhelmingly toward the second choice, but the very fact that the second response even enlists careful consideration illustrates the point: the most unprofessional personal appeal can favorably compete with the most professional impersonal appeal. The most successful nonprofit organizations will continue to be those that encourage around them cultivation of the broadest and deepest personal relationships.

Sacrificial Giving Will Continue to Be Confined to the Non-Affluent

In over a quarter of a century of working in the nonprofit sector and in encounters with thousands of others in that community, I have never heard of a confirmed case of a sacrificial gift from a very wealthy person.

To be clear, I mean by "sacrificial" a gift that forces a significant and fundamental lifestyle change upon the donor (as opposed to one, however admirable, that changes how someone *might* otherwise live, or that follows a lifestyle change that was otherwise contemplated). I know of many sacrificial gifts from the non-affluent along the lines of the Biblical account of the "widow's mite." And the fact that I don't know of such gifts from among the very affluent doesn't, of course, mean that they don't occur; I strongly suspect they do. I yearn and expect some day to be told of such gifts. But they must be very rare. So, despite my optimism stated earlier in this chapter that giving will significantly improve, I don't imagine that it will mean the wealthiest among us will give until they can't give any more. According to *Giving USA*, the wealthiest 1 percent of the population currently gives an average of 1.3 percent to charity. I hope and expect that percentage will increase, but even a doubling of giving among that classification of donor will not cause for its members significant new sacrifices.

Conclusion

My grandmother described her perspective on the Great Depression as a horizon with a low-set sun. Depending upon where you stood and when you were looking, it might seem at the moment to be either dawn or dusk. I find it a useful image for today's world, which, we are reminded, is cyclical and enduring. In the chapters of this book, wise and wonderful professionals I am privileged to count as colleagues at Skystone Ryan seek to shed light on particular patches of the changing philanthropic world. It is a world we are blessed to inhabit. It is a new day we gladly welcome.

A Person of Influence, A Sculptor of the Universe

How Women Are Changing the Face of Philanthropy

LISA BARNWELL WILLIAMS

During a recent reunion with a colleague from my first development job, conversation turned to the woman who, as a board member and capital campaign chair, led the first major fundraising project in each of our careers. We joked about her perfume and her parties, but our nostalgia left me wondering.

Mrs. R., as we can call her, was a tiny woman but a very large presence. Wife of a local industrialist, she was from a modest background and lived her late-life affluence to the maximum, with a spectacular and luxurious home, colorful, high-fashion clothing, and a carefully cultivated aura of celebrity and glamour. Staff and volunteers alike presumed that the capital campaign she chaired was just another social achievement for Mrs. R, another way for her to use her husband's money to buy recognition, status, and respect. If that was the goal, she was certainly successful: the principal building constructed with campaign funds bears her name.

In hindsight, however, I'm ashamed of our collective response to Mrs. R. Like all my colleagues, I underestimated her. Her commitment to the campaign and its objectives was real and heartfelt. I often tell clients in the early stages of campaign planning that the ideal chair wakes up every morning wondering how the campaign will do that day, and Mrs. R. is one of the very few chairs I've known who really was that engaged. Furthermore, the campaign she chaired was successful. In the face of some very substantial hurdles—staff turnover, unanticipated financial needs, local politics—volunteers stayed on task, gifts both large and small were secured, the goal was reached on schedule, and the campaign initiatives were executed. Even at the time, I realized that the collective energy was sustained largely by Mrs. R.'s sometimes-annoying dedication and drive. Not until many years later did I develop the perspective to recognize that her single-minded focus on the need and her relentless and strategic pursuit of every potential leadership donor set the example and laid the foundation that enabled the campaign to succeed.

In short, I, like my colleagues, viewed Mrs. R. through the lens that inevitably colored the picture of women in philanthropy just one generation ago. Despite the formal roles she played in the organization and the campaign, her pacesetting generosity, and her personal achievements, she was seen mainly as an adjunct to her husband, as a social creature pursuing not the official and collective goals but her own personal ones, and as a free agent operating outside the organizational structure. Somehow, we overlooked her accomplishments as a big-league donor, a powerful, effective fundraiser, and an inspirational leader.

Having moved cross-country since we worked together, I don't know whether Mrs. R., probably now in her eighties, is still engaged in philanthropic activities. I hope so, because the philanthropic world is ready for her now.

Women Are in the Game

It should come as no surprise that women's role in philanthropy has increased along with our increasing financial power. After all, responsibility for charity has been in the female domain for centuries. Bake sales, Ladies' Auxiliaries, and casseroles delivered to the sick: the scale is small, but the motives are indisputably philanthropic.

By assuming an active role in the world of commerce and finance, women have, during the past few decades, developed both the capacity and the confidence to translate the female tradition of small-scale charity to a larger stage. Statistics draw a clear picture of the changing role. Women are engaged in the business world to an extent barely imagined not so very long ago:

- More than 60 percent of women are in the workplace, compared with half that number in 1950.
- Women's median income has increased more than 60 percent over the past 30 years, a period during which men's median income remained largely stable.
- Some two-fifths of privately held U.S. businesses are majority-female owned, with 10.1 million businesses employing 13 million people, according to the Center for Women's Business Research.
- The 2008–2009 recession affected men more than women; dramatic slowdowns in historically male fields such as construction and manufacturing coupled with the relative strength of traditionally female industries like health care and government led to unprecedented male/female parity in the workforce.

Women are expected to control 60 percent of all private wealth in the United States in 2010, and we make 80 percent of all purchases. The much-discussed generational wealth transfer taking place over the next 40 years will disproportionately impact women, who will inherit 70 percent of the $41 trillion transferred, according to Boston College's Center on Wealth and Philanthropy.

The consequent scaling-up of women's giving is equally apparent through the numbers. Accounting firm Grant Thornton's analysis of Internal Revenue Service data reveals that women donated

Women have the same core motivations for giving as men—altruism, gratitude, the desire to make a better world . . . however, women approach giving differently than men, just as they have different styles of communication and management.

—Women's Philanthropy Institute

more than men in 2005, $21.7 billion compared with male donors' $16.8 billion. As a percentage of wealth, the discrepancy is even more marked; a recently released report by Barclay's Wealth shows that while men in the United States give an average of 1.8 percent of their wealth, women give nearly twice as much, an average of 3.5 percent. Women's control over the charitable sphere is reflected also in the influence they wield over their husbands' gifts; a recent study by Fidelity Charitable Gift Fund reveals that more women than men assume primary or sole responsibility in determining how much to donate and which charities to support, and that 92 percent of men indicate that their charitable decisions are influenced by their spouses.

The Fidelity study is revealing also in its analysis of the motivations and emotional factors that distinguish men's and women's philanthropic behavior. The study of high-income, $1,000+ donors (the participants' average total giving in 2008 was $6,600) reveals that:

- Only 42 percent of women, compared with 54 percent of all donors, prefer that their gifts remain anonymous.
- More women than men have used innovative giving mechanisms such as private foundations and donor-advised funds.
- More than one-third of women, compared with one-quarter of men, indicate that they expect to give more in "challenging economic times."
- Significantly more women than men place their charitable giving in the context of family tradition, including a strong commitment to passing a charitable legacy along to their children.

The study also identifies psychographic categories to describe the behavior of groups of donors. Just over half the donors studied are identified as Mainstream Givers, predominantly male donors who, reflecting the stereotype of conservative philanthropy, give regularly and predictably to a set group of recipients. Two of the other three identified groups, both predominately women, reveal characteristics that are instructive as we seek to characterize the impact that women's increasing involvement in philanthropy will have on nonprofit organizations:

Empathetic Givers, 29 percent of the total, give more on average than Mainstream Givers, and give in response to perceived need. They also volunteer more and value family engagement in philanthropy.

Pioneering Givers, 4 percent of the total, give the largest amount on average and also the largest as a percentage of income. Typically younger than other donors, they are the only group to identify themselves as philanthropists. They are cause-oriented and open to innovative giving strategies.

A recent Center on Philanthropy study on generations, gender, and giving reinforces these behavioral patterns. In addition to investigating generational factors and the role of education, religion, and marital factors, researchers observe that women are more likely than men to give for these core reasons:

- To help meet the basic needs of the very poor.
- To help the poor help themselves.
- To fulfill a responsibility to help those with less.
- To make the world better (a particularly strong motivator among younger women).

The givers in both these surveys clearly manifest many of the "The 6 Cs: Women's Motivations for Giving" that Martha Taylor and Sondra Shaw-Hardy describe in their pioneering work with the Women's Philanthropy Institute at the Center on Philanthropy. As first published in *Reinventing Fundraising: Realizing the Potential of Women's Fundraising* in 1995, women use their philanthropic endeavors to:

- Create
  - Women want to create new solutions to problems.
  - Women like to be entrepreneurial with their philanthropy.
- Change
  - Women give to make a difference.
  - Women are less interested in providing unrestricted support to preserve the status quo of an organization or institution.

- Connect
  - Women prefer to see the human face their gift affects.
  - Women want to build a partnership with people connected with the project they fund.
- Commit
  - Women commit to organizations and institutions whose vision they share.
  - Women often give to the organization for which they have volunteered.
- Collaborate
  - Women prefer to work with others as part of a larger effort.
  - Women seek to avoid duplication, competition, and waste.
- Celebrate
  - Women seek to celebrate their accomplishments, have fun together, and enjoy the deeper meaning and satisfaction of their philanthropy.

There's Power in Numbers

The recurring theme in the many 2009 media reports on women's philanthropy is the extent to which, for women, giving is a community activity. The rapid growth of women's funds, giving circles, and similar gender-specific philanthropic mechanisms attests to the communitarian needs and motivations of many women donors. It is astonishing to realize that until the founding of the Ms. Foundation for Women in 1972, women's philanthropy did not exist as a formal phenomenon.

Women's community giving initiatives today take many forms, from small, casual neighborhood-based circles to multi-million dollar international funds. The Women's Funding Network, a coalition of 135 women's funds around the world, serves as a nexus for a broad range of foundations and funds focused on women's giving. Ranging from the

We believe that every gift has the ability to empower its donor and inspire our whole movement.

—Women's Funding Network
2008 Annual Report

broad scope and deep pockets of the Global Fund for Women, which has given $47 million in 162 countries since 1987 to special purposes and religiously affiliated foundations to women-focused funds on every continent and community funds in cities and states across the United States, the members of the Women's Funding Network collectively control $465 million in working assets (2008), and invest $60 million annually in women and girls.

The first women's funds, in the 1970s, were responsible for drawing attention and resources to important issues that had, until that time, been largely swept under the societal rug—among them domestic violence, economic inequality, and reproductive rights. Over time, the range of issues addressed has broadened, coming to enable cross-cultural, cross-national, cross-class communication about a wide diversity of other concerns that have a special impact on women and girls. The slogan "Think globally, act locally" could have been invented to describe women's funds, as the patchwork of programs and organizations supported—local, regional, national or international—come together to address many of the major issues of our time: health, human rights, and economic security. These funds allow women as donors (although not all donors to women's funds are women, of course) to direct their dollars toward women's issues.

As an example of the multileveled ways in which a women's fund can simultaneously enrich donors, grant recipients, and an entire community, The Women's Fund of the Greater Cincinnati Foundation, founded with a $5,000 gift in 1995, has seen its mission and programs evolve over time. Grantmaking was, as expected, the initial focus and remains a central priority. Over time, however, the Fund has assumed a "think tank" role as well, gathering research and shaping thought about issues pertaining to women and girls in the region. The first of these studies, completed in 2005, provided among other things the foundation for the Fund's current agenda:

- *Close the gap*—Reduce disparities faced by women of color, women in poverty, and women heading households alone.
- *Grow strong girls*—Increase opportunities for girls to connect with their families, peers, school, and community.

- *Develop women leaders*—Lead collaborations that increase leadership development, networking, and mentoring.
- *Assess progress*—Support opportunities to improve the collection of gender-specific data.

This agenda, in turn, forms the strategic basis for The Women's Fund's various funds, campaigns, and grant initiatives, including a number of named funds as well as the Voices of Leadership Campaign; the Economic Security Initiative Fund; the Developing Women & Girls Leadership Fund; the Women's Fund General Pool; and The Cincinnati Business and Professional Women Scholarship Fund.

Let's Get Together and Give!

If their layered impacts and broad perspectives make women's funds the gold standard of the collective power of women as givers, giving circles are the local currencies. The giving circle movement, informally launched in 1995 with the founding of The Washington Women's Foundation, is a vigorous recent manifestation of the communitarian giving and mutual aid themes that recur so frequently in American history, sharing features not only with many women's funds but also with social venture philanthropy initiatives such as Social Venture Partners.

I have found that among its other benefits, giving liberates the soul of the giver.

—Maya Angelou

The giving circle model encompasses groups that vary widely in size, composition, affiliation, practice, and objective, but share these fundamental criteria:

- Donors pool their resources in some manner.
- The donors decide how and where the funds are distributed.
- There is an educational and/or community building component to the circle.[1]

The number of participants in a circle can range from just a few—many groups choose to remain small enough to meet in a living room or around a dining room table—to several hundred. The most common model requires an equivalent dollar commitment from all participants, enabling all members in turn to participate equally in the research and grantmaking processes. The annual commitments seem most often to be in the $500 to $2,500 range, but there are circles that require gifts as small as $25 or as large as $50,000. Less commonly, the level of commitment is not defined, allowing circles to be more diverse in age, income, and ethnicity and, potentially, more represent-ative of the community. Circles using this approach typically structure their operations carefully to avoid stratification and ensure equal participation of members regardless of contribution level.

There has to be a connection between the donor and the recipient. I call it a heart connection. People need to feel and know where their money is going. The problems of this world can be solved by connecting those in need to those with resources.

—Julie Fisher Cummings
Lovelight Foundation as quoted in "Women's Giving Circles: Reflections from the Founders"

At least 400 giving circles currently exist across the nation, and experts project that there may be twice that many, with the number doubling each year for much of the current decade. They involve tens of thousands of donors and have made grants estimated at $100 million or more since 2000. Some are informal, operating with no formal structure; some are independent 501(c)(3) organizations; and many are hosted by other organizations, including community foundations and women's funds.

The vast majority of giving circles have sprouted autonomously since the late 1990s, often the mission of a single, motivated founder, many inspired by examples in other communities and by coverage of the phenomenon in the media, including pieces in *People* and *Real Simple* magazines. A few community foundations have chosen to shepherd the birth of giving circles, and New Ventures in Philan-thropy, an initiative of the Forum of Regional Associations of Grant-makers, encouraged the formation of circles through the Baltimore

Giving Project, Giving New England, Giving Greater Chicago, and Minnesota Council on Foundations. Even those circles created under the auspices of larger organizations, however, depend on the commitment of individual leaders. Relying on members' interests and commitments to spark community involvement and on personal networks for recruitment, a giving circle must be member-driven to succeed.

Contrary to the popular image, giving circles are not exclusively female. Some estimates suggest that fewer than one in five circles involve men, but the survey sample studied by the Forum of Regional Associations of Grantmakers was only 57 percent female. Regardless of gender composition, as a phenomenon, the circles adhere very closely to "The 6 Cs" of women's giving outlined previously, and as such reflect many of the special characteristics of women as donors:

- Create

   Giving circles are by their very nature entrepreneurial; not only are the circles themselves new organizations created explicitly to meet a charitable need, but their grantmaking is commonly creative and "out of the box."
- Change

   Most giving circles see themselves as change agents, synergistically mobilizing the power—financial and otherwise—of the individual participants to effect social change.
- Connect

   Many circles focused on local giving include visits to or presentations by potential grant recipients as part of their grantmaking process. Others, including those with an international focus, use research and education to develop members' in-depth, personal understanding of issues, organizations, and needs.
- Commit

   The hands-on research and education practices of most giving circles encourage members to become immersed in the issues, identify with the organizations that address them, and become champions for action.

- Collaborate

  Clearly, collaboration is the very essence of giving circles—shared goals, shared decision making, and the power of joining together.

- Celebrate

  Giving circles commonly underscore the celebratory aspect of giving, sometimes choosing to limit membership rather than give up meeting in members' homes or sharing meals.

Some may be surprised that, unlike women's funds and despite the predominance of women in the movement, giving circle grantmaking is not heavily focused on issues that directly impact women and girls. That is one of several common priorities, but the circles' financial support targets also the broad topics and concerns that many studies have identified as the typical motivators for female donors: youth, human services, and crisis intervention.

Many women come to us not knowing much about philanthropy, not having been that purposeful about where they're giving their money. . . . With us, for the first time, these women are deciding to focus their charitable giving . . .

—Hali Lee
Asian Women's Giving Circle as quoted in "Women's Giving Circles: Reflections from the Founders"

Like the women's funds discussed above, giving circles benefit the donor as well as the recipient. Many giving circles engage with community needs in ways that go beyond grantmaking. Organized volunteer activities, board-level involvement, and individual financial support for recipient organizations are common. Educational activities, both structured and informal, are also common, exposing members to learning opportunities ranging from issue-oriented presentations by nonprofits to grantsmanship training.

Women's giving—particularly in the high-engagement, collaborative environment of the giving circle or the women's fund—grows women donors. Cultivating philanthropists is an explicit mission objective of many circles; the required membership donation is often defined as a stretch goal and is expected to be the largest gift a member has made. Educational offerings and peer-to-peer sharing reinforce the philanthropic impulse and provide both example and instruction to further empower and embolden circle members. That these efforts are successful is implied by statistics suggesting that nearly 70 percent of giving circle participants give additional money directly to the nonprofits that the circles fund. In addition, studies have shown that the education offered by giving circles combined with the hands-on experience of large-scale grantmaking makes circle members more thoughtful, strategic, and generous in their personal giving.

Moving onto the Big Stage

Recently, the goal of growing female philanthropists has leaped to public consciousness through the success of a high-level, high-visibility initiative with the very frank intention of transforming the face of philanthropy. Women Moving Millions (WMM), a collaboration between the Women's Funding Network, its member foundations, and 100 (and counting) individual donors, has achieved a two-fold goal: targeting substantial funding to programs and organizations to improve the lives of women and girls, and inspiring female donors at the million-dollar level.

> *These women have been timid. They have always been charitable, but compared to women of lesser means, their gifts have not been generous. We are challenging them to do their part, and make a real difference.*
>
> —Ambassador Swanee Hunt
> Co-Founder, Women
> Moving Millions

Created in 2006 by sisters Swanee Hunt and Helen LaKelly Hunt, Women Moving Millions aims to mobilize those "Pioneering Givers" identified in the Fidelity study discussed above: women who are cause-oriented and open to innovative giving strategies. And, of course, capable of making a seven-figure commitment. The very particular demographic of high-net-worth women who have, for the most part, not yet been major philanthropic players has responded enthusiastically to Women Moving Millions, exceeding the initiative's $150 million goal to raise $176 million by May 2009.

Beyond their basic demographic descriptors, the Women Moving Millions participants are a diverse lot, 98 women (and 2 men) who have come to philanthropy by a variety of winding roads. And the roads they have followed are a key part of the WMM strategy. Press accounts of the initiative, as well as the Women Moving Millions Web site, have focused on the stories of the women involved. The stories provide an important context for the gifts and the givers, lending a face to the sometimes abstract concept of the million-dollar gift.

The quantitative success of the Women Moving Millions initiative attests to the effectiveness of this storytelling strategy in engaging and inspiring the target audience—women capable of top-level philanthropy. In addition, however, the donor stories make the initiative much more effective than it might otherwise have been as a role model for women's giving overall. WMM has constructed a virtual community that is in some ways a reflection of a giving circle: a group of women who know one another (at least by virtue of their published stories) and join together in philanthropy. Reading the personal stories of WMM donors who illustrate concepts like Courage, Bold, Reach, and Spark allows and encourages any woman, regardless of means, to see herself as a member of that generous club.

Who Are the Women on Your Team?

Particularly at a time of increased financial pressures and growing competition for donors, nonprofit organizations of every kind are asking what they can do to attract female donors. As with most aspects of fundraising, there is no one right answer. To develop an effective strategy, each organization must look inside at its history, its mission, its leadership, its constituency, its community, and its giving traditions. Do you know who gives to you, and why? And perhaps equally important, who rarely gives to you, and why not?

As noted above, there is substantial research suggesting that women give differently than men. The motives for giving are different, the expectations of the supported organization are different, and the definitions of "stewardship" are different. Becoming familiar with the growing body of research on women's philan-thropic behavior is certainly wise and prudent. Offering opportuni-ties for collaborative, hands-on giving; reinforcing community values and family traditions; addressing human needs and youth and family issues—the many studies we have discussed provide important start-ing points for any organization seeking a more intentional, strategic approach to women donors.

But to presume that the research says all we need to know is to risk a replay of my 1980s experience with Mrs. R.: allowing assumptions and generalizations to overshadow the real behaviors of real donors in real organizations. Just as your organization is distinctive in ways both large and small, different even from other organizations with similar mis-sion and scope, your donors, female and male, are different as well.

So, as a first step, look at your organization. Look at your board. Are they diverse in gender and in other characteristics? Are women in leadership roles? Are certain tasks segregated, by convention if not officially? For example, many organizations, even to-day, default to traditions that place men as finance com-mittee chairs and women as gala chairs. You can imagine the message this sends to the female financier who may be a potential donor!

Consumer research has demonstrated how loyal women are to the products they buy. That same loyalty shapes their charitable behavior.

—Vanessa Freytag
Executive Director
The Women's Fund of the Greater
Cincinnati Foundation

Look at your volunteer structures. Are they gender-neutral? Conventionally organized guilds and auxiliaries can make room for men without changing their names or their traditions. At the same time, gender-specific volunteer traditions—for instance, coach-ing or grounds maintenance as male activities, special events or classroom support as female activities—can be difficult to overcome unless the formal volunteer structures are carefully mindful of gender issues. Are volunteers integrated into the organization's overall stew-ardship program? Some organizations, particularly those traditionally supported by women volunteers, segregate volunteers from donors, and if volunteers are never asked, they can hardly be expected to give generously. More effective programs acknowledge the deep commitment volunteers can feel to an organization and provide opportunities for giving in various ways, including planned gifts, that respect that commitment regardless of financial capabilities.

Look at your donors. An analytic assessment, formal or informal, can give you insights into their age, gender, ethnicity, geographic location, relationship to your organization, and so forth. Are your donors alumni, or members, or ticket buyers, or are they wholly distinct from your beneficiaries (as for a food bank or homeless shelter, for example)? Do most donors give year after year?

Look at your major donors, asking many of the same questions. Do their gifts recur from year to year? Do they increase? Are the major donors engaged in other roles, as board members or volunteers? Are there opportunities for them to be involved?

This introspection is appropriate and necessary as a precursor to any thoughtful effort to enrich an organization's development program. How do the resulting insights help to refine a strategic approach to women as a special constituency?

> *The moment a woman comes home to herself, the moment she knows that she has become a person of influence, an artist of her life, a sculptor of the universe, a person with rights and responsibilities who is respected and recognized, the resurrection of the world begins.*
>
> —Joan Chittister, OSB

Here's a radical notion: Ask the women. Recruit some female leaders in your organization and your community to serve as a steering committee, taking the lead in developing a strategy not only for attracting female donors, but for developing coherent, sustainable programs for donor engagement, recognition, and retention. Focus groups might provide an opportunity to hear directly from women constituents, and, depending on their responses, the steering committee might consider a variety of strategic approaches. Among the models used by nonprofit organizations of various kinds and sizes are:

- An organization-specific giving circle, allowing members to evaluate options and determine how the funds will be allocated.

- A women-only major gift club, in which members solicit other members.
- A leadership council that advocates for women's issues within the organization, provides leadership roles, and perhaps includes mentorship opportunities.
- A topical support organization that engages women in an area of interest, offering both opportunities for support and content-specific programming.
- A women-only campaign.

There are many outstanding examples of institutional initiatives to promote and reward women's philanthropy, and your steering committee might want to do some research or take a field trip or two to see some programs in action. In higher education, the University of Wisconsin was a pioneer, targeting women for major gifts through the Women's Philanthropy Council since the virtually prehistoric year 1988. The University of Mississippi, Virginia Tech, the University of Kentucky, and the University of South Florida, among others, frame their women's giving program into a context of leadership and mentorship, and allocate the funds thus raised to scholarships. The giving circle model is used in several institutions, including the University of Tennessee and Ohio State, Ball State, and Arizona State Universities, allowing participants to give at a set level, then collaborate with other members to determine how their collective gifts will be used. Ohio University has a hybrid program, with multiple giving circles supporting different areas of university life, and the University of Minnesota's giving circle model includes among its giving levels a $100 per year option for current students. Iowa State University and the University of Virginia have folded their women and philanthropy initiatives into capital campaigns, focusing on campaign leadership and recognition of women's current and historic roles.

Several national organizations have seeded women's initiatives that are blooming in chapters nationwide. Led by the United Way America's Women's Leadership Council, local United Ways in communities of every size, in every region, have launched solicitation and recognition programs that focus on women.

Jewish communities and federations, long welcoming women in leadership roles, are also leaders in women's philanthropy. A recent United Jewish Communities Report observes that Women's Philanthropy campaigns are the fastest-growing component of the annual campaign, accounting for 22 percent of the total; many local campaigns are even more dependent on women, as at The Jewish Federation of Seattle, where the Women in Philanthropy initiative is responsible for generating one-third of the annual Community Campaign. Other initiatives, such as the Lion of Judah endowment's focus on deferred gifts and Jewish Women's Foundations that focus on gender-specific issues and needs, provide multiple opportunities for women donors within the constellation of Jewish charities.

Other nonprofit organizations with solid structures in place to coordinate women's giving range from the American Red Cross, whose Tiffany Circle recognizes $10,000 donors to local chapters with high-end recognition, including a signature Tiffany pin, to small local hospitals that have facilitated the transformation of traditional volunteer guilds into powerfully philanthropic women's boards and philanthropy circles.

Which of these many models is appropriate for your organization? Listen to your data, listen to your constituents, and listen to your volunteer leadership. One size does not fit all.

While much of the energy surrounding women in philanthropy is focused on top-level gifts and givers, it is important to keep in mind that giving is not the special preserve of the very affluent. Indeed, recent research indicates that women with annual incomes of less than $10,000 give an amazing 5.4 percent of their adjusted gross income to charity—a much higher percentage than women overall, and nearly three times as high a percentage as men. For lower-income donors, commitment is the key. I will never forget a woman I encountered while consulting for an organization that served victims of domestic violence. A domestic violence survivor herself, she was hardly wealthy but appeared year after year as one of the agency's leadership donors—because she committed nearly 25 percent of her annual salary to a mission she was passionate about.

Attention to ways of giving is critical to lower-income donors, and relevant to women giving at any level. Simple devices like monthly payment plans and credit card payments can make it easier for a woman (or anyone) to make a stretch gift. And, thanks to the communitarian impulse that helps guide many women's giving, female donors are often particularly responsive to challenges and matching gifts. Planned giving prospects are frequently overlooked when an organization assesses its donor potential. The prototypical planned giving prospect is an older, single woman, typically of modest income but with considerable assets derived from savings or inheritance. Without a history of leadership-level giving, these potential supporters can be nearly invisible within an organization. Yet statistics show that a majority of charitable bequest donors are women, and nearly half of women with estates of $5 million or more leave a charitable bequest, compared with only one-third of similarly wealthy men.

A special word of encouragement is due those organizations whose missions fall outside the women and girls/human service continuum that is in the forefront of women's giving. Reviewing the data on women's giving patterns and preferences, one would think that there are no female donors to the arts, for instance. Again, generalizations are risky—even generalizations supported by data. All of us can name innumerable women engaged at the highest levels of organizations in the arts or environmental causes or health care, from committed volunteers to board leaders to major donors. The WHY of any gift is the donor's commitment to the mission: Your donors, and your volunteers and board members, are committed. To develop the women in your constituency as givers, focus on the HOW, to maximize the commitment that already exists.

Women need to know all the details. No matter how busy they are, they still want to be hands-on.

—M. Anne Abbe
Associate Vice President for
Development
University of North Texas

Developing programs to target women donors is potentially rewarding, but it is an ambitious and demanding undertaking.

The engagement, connection, and creativity that women seek in giving require a substantially higher level of involvement from the organization. Managing even a few top-tier female donors can be time-consuming; working with giving circles is famously demanding, as the groups typically seek a comprehensive understanding of virtually every aspect of potential grantees. Sustained attention and involvement is essential to any relationship-based work, and women's programming is no different. A comprehensive, long-term calendar of events, dedicated staff, active volunteer leadership: A substantial infrastructure is required to mobilize a women in philanthropy program.

Every organization must decide for itself how much investment is merited, or even possible. Clearly any nonprofit with a small staff and limited resources must think very carefully before committing to any new ongoing program.

Conclusion

No investment is necessary, however, to develop a thoughtful, strategic approach to women as donors. Women are the majority of the population. We make the majority of purchases, control the majority of assets, own nearly half the businesses, and make most of the charitable gifts. The demographics of the nonprofit world suggest that it is very likely that if you are reading this paragraph, you are a woman. Women are no longer content to take a passive or invisible role in philanthropy, as Sondra Shaw-Hardy and Martha Taylor note in their updated "Three Cs for the 21st Century: The Results of Women's Giving":

- Control
  - Women are taking control of their lives, their finances, and their philanthropy.
- Confidence
  - Women have gained the confidence to become philanthropic leaders.
- Courage
  - Women have the courage to challenge the old way of doing things and take risks with their giving to bring about change.

Building Strong Nonprofits

Female philanthropists are everywhere, from the million-dollar donor to Women Moving Millions to the young professional getting together with her giving circle to the low-income woman donating $45 of her $800 per month income to my old friend Mrs. R. Every organization can, and must, acknowledge and respect the power that women, as individuals and together, bring to the communities they believe in.

CHAPTER 3

The New Nonprofit

How Human Nature, Business Principles, and Financial Realities are Transforming the Missions, Management, and Finance of Nonprofit Organizations

CHARLEY ANSBACH

The earth has moved under nonprofit organizations. How they are managed, financed, and measured for success is changing. Exceptions aside, running a successful nonprofit

> *It is not the strongest of the species that survives, nor the most intelligent, but the one most responsive to change.*
>
> —Charles Darwin

or social benefit corporation in the coming years will never quite be the same.

A Period of Significant Change in the Nonprofit Sector

Today, organizations that fail to address the changes going on around them run the risk of being seen in the rearview mirror of community service, education, health care, and every other facet of nonprofit service. Established groups as well as ones newly formed that follow the established traditions of nonprofit management, finance, and service will be challenged or surpassed by those that are figuring out new ways to solve social issues more effectively and sustainably. Nonprofits that embrace new management models will be better positioned to:

- Produce more and better results for each dollar invested.
- Find new ways to engage donors more fully.
- Diversify funding streams and more often include earned income.
- Brand their services and communicate their messages more professionally.
- Produce measurable results that are meaningful to their donor investors.
- Approach their missions in a scalable manner sufficient to solve—rather than simply maintain—the community problems and opportunities they were formed to address.

How have donor attitudes changed? Private donors in general are no longer as willing or able to fund an unlimited and often redundant array of nonprofit services. Nor does government have sufficient funds to meet all of the needs of the community at the scale to which those needs have grown and at the level of quality that is now expected. Private foundations in general have temporarily lost a portion of their corpus funding and, despite the creation of a few mega foundations, do not have sufficient funds to fill the gap created by the cutbacks in government spending and individual giving, nor is there the desire or intent to do so. Many companies have all but eliminated their community giving programs, and the funding that is available now is lodged in their marketing offices that are intrinsically resistant to traditional fundraising appeals.

What are the new nonprofit models? Earned income, value proposition-based partnerships with for-profit companies, partnerships and mergers with other nonprofits, and public/private partnerships with government represent examples on a growing list of sustainability considerations available to nonprofit organizations. These options are largely uncharted territory for nonprofits to consider, let alone manage effectively. Nevertheless, that is where many new opportunities for survival and future growth for nonprofits and social benefit organizations will be found.

How will organizations know if they are falling behind the curve of change? Donors will begin to lose interest because they are not involved or do not see sufficient value resulting from their investments. Board members begin to leave and cannot be replaced because they do not feel comfortable with the method of management. And, perhaps most importantly, recipients or users of their services do not enjoy or otherwise benefit at the levels that they, like donors, consider meaningful.

Perhaps one of the most visible indicators as to whether an organization is staying current with the times, managing itself well, and maintaining the interest of its investors, partners, and customers is money. The health of an organization's donated or earned income can reveal its relevance. The old chestnuts like "No money, no mission" remain germane. More effective management and ways to track performance are now critical factors to consider and address.

At the same time, there will always be exceptions. Dedicated leaders and volunteers often see dire needs in the community long before or in spite of the absence of any funding to help solve them. By dint of will, passion, and commitment, they work tirelessly to solve those problems against all odds. Thankfully, it appears that will never change. However, it is when those causes turn into ongoing organizations that issues such as better management become relevant.

> *Business as usual (for nonprofit organizations) is out. . . . This is the time for creativity and innovation.*
>
> —Diana Aviv, President
> Independent Sector in
> *Chronicle of Philanthropy*
> April 27, 2009

What is the effect of the new economy? The global economic crisis of 2008–2009 threw a management wild card into the operational hand of the nonprofit community. Some very worthy organizations began to disappear because there just is not enough money available from established sources to support their missions regardless of how well they carry them out. This is happening in cities all across the country. For example, in San Francisco at the start of 2008, there were more than 7,000 registered 501(c)3 social benefit corporations (nonprofits) operating in that city. Together, those organizations represented over

7.7 percent of the wages paid locally. Shortly after the start of the recession, the media predicted that more than one-third of those nonprofits would close. In that case, the closures would not necessarily mean they all lacked some important management quality, but rather that there simply was not enough donor support, ticket buyers, or public contracts available to keep them all going in difficult financial times. It remains to be seen if those predictions were overly zealous.

At the same time, it is important to note that despite the difficult economic conditions a group of new organizations and initiatives, as well as some old organizations with innovative programs and leadership, are doing reasonably well. Why? It is not luck.

Change or die. One reason may be that some organizations adapt faster and better to change than others. Alan Deutschman's book *Change or Die* explores the concept that faced with even the direst outcome, the loss of their own life due to conditions that they personally have the power to change, people tend not to alter those behaviors regardless of the inevitable result. The author goes on to report that research to determine what it would take to get people to act in their own best interests found, generally speaking, that it can be done but it takes an organized, sustained effort. Many nonprofit organizations find themselves in a similar "change or die" situation. Changes often are needed in order to become more effective and sustainable, and there are methods available for making those changes. The question is which organizations will do what is necessary and sustain those actions over time in order to prosper.

Why Are Things Changing?

The recent financial crisis certainly accelerated the need for doing things differently among nonprofit organizations, but it did not start there. While there is no specific "moment" in which this present atmosphere of change began, in hindsight, donor attitudes and responses could have provided us the first glimmer that is was beginning to happen.

Over the last decade or two it was common to hear major gifts officers and capital campaign managers offhandedly talking about an attitude shift among some of their more significant donors.

Donors were becoming increasingly interested in return on invest-ment (donation) and programmatic outcomes. Some of the most persistent themes were, for example:

- Irritation at increasing—and seemingly out of control—requests for funds to pay rising costs of doing service.
- Wasteful duplication of services in the geographic area.
- Little or no measurable progress toward solving the problem the organization has committed itself to address, which in-spired little hope and aroused suspicion about effectiveness.
- Frustration at development and administrative or "middleman" layers that added costs but provided no direct benefit to the target population.

In general, donors began to express their frustration over what they perceived as inefficient management, a lack of accountability, and an absence of clear results among nonprofits. Some talked about wanting to get more involved but in some new, yet-to-be-defined ways other than joining another board or committee. Add to that a few highly visible scandals involving nonprofit executives caught in financial mismanagement and the atmosphere for a perfect storm of change began to form.

Some Things Are Not Changing

Mission is key. The mission of each nonprofit organization is still its anchor. Mission drift, usually brought about when a group is chasing money, still is the condition to avoid. By contrast, mission "update" is becoming an important if not essential tool in building the basis for sustainability in the coming years.

Donors continue to give. Millions of people still want to help others and are willing to donate, volunteer, and participate in the well-being of their communities, as well as their country and the world as a whole. Despite the economy, many nonprofits have seen annual giving remain steady and in some cases even grow. Major gift and capital campaigns slowed and even stopped altogether in many areas of the country recently but appear to be back on the rise, albeit slowly.

Generosity, it is gratifying to note, appears to be a reliable human quality.

Nurturing donors is still important. Donors still tend to invest the most money into causes and organizations where they feel the greatest sense of personal connection and involvement, as well as see the greatest returns on their investments. Kay Sprinkle-Grace describes this relationship well in her book, *Beyond Fundraising.* For donors, returns on investment still come in several forms: the personal satisfaction involved, the social benefit produced, the recognition received, and the business and social connections that can result. Therefore, donor recognition remains an important part of keeping supporters engaged, which in turn is the lifeblood of most organizations.

Qualified and willing staff members are interested in the nonprofit world. There is an established and growing corps of community service professionals who, despite the generally lower-than-normal pay rates and the higher-than-normal time demands involved, remain dedicated to working in the nonprofit sector. More and more students in MBA programs and other disciplines in colleges and universities are expressing an interest in building their careers in the nonprofit field. The study of social entrepreneurism is becoming particularly attractive. Similarly, there is a small but steady flow of successful for-profit executives who continue to explore switching careers to get involved in the nonprofit sector. Lastly, as in other times of financial difficulty, the recent global recession has caused job seekers from all industries to begin looking for opportunities wherever they can find them, including the nonprofit sector.

Nonprofit organizations continue to be formed. According to the Foundation Center, in 1988 there were 900,000 registered tax-exempt nonprofit social benefit corporations in the United States. By 2009 there were over 1.5 million and thousands more non-governmental organizations (NGOs) operating around the world. Those organizations in the United States had over $1.7 trillion in revenues. There is no real way to predict how this sector will look coming out of the global recession, but there appears to be little doubt it will continue to exist and grow in sync with the rest of the economy, whatever that may be.

Leadership can be slow to adapt to external forces. Another unchanging feature of this sector is how slowly many nonprofits tend to notice and deal with external change, regardless of the difficulty that the subsequent delay may cause for them and their missions. Generally speaking, it is safe to say that until now many staff and volunteers in nonprofit organizations came from the social service field and approached the running of a nonprofit organization as secondary to doing good in the community. It is a feature that may have been laudable but is now potentially lethal in terms of maintaining long-term relevance and sustainability.

Familiarity with donor-driven charity limits financial innovation. The donor-driven charity finance model has been and continues to be the most familiar and deeply ingrained management approach in the nonprofit culture. It is the model best known to board members, staff, volunteers, donors, media, regulatory agencies, and the public at large. Despite a great deal of information, successful models, and pressure from individual board members and donors to the contrary, many nonprofit groups continue to fear that using other finance and management models, such as earned income and partnerships, will jeopardize their nonprofit, social benefit corporation tax exempt status. While there are limits imposed by tax law that must be addressed, much of this managerial reluctance is based not on fact but instead on habit, hesitancy, and comfort with the familiar, as well as the lack of time to learn new skills.

Perceived culture conflict prevents board members from leveraging skills. Even the most seasoned business executives may leave their business brains at the door when they join a nonprofit board. Simply make that statement in a group of nonprofit leaders, and you will see enough heads nodding affirmatively to know the assertion is correct. One reason for-profit business leaders tend to apply their experience only marginally to their role as nonprofit board members could be called the conflict of cultures. "Nonprofit" has for years been widely taken to mean that tax-exempt organizations should not have surplus income, and earned revenues were most likely out of sync with the sector's moral and legal guidelines. The whole idea was to take on community causes that were important but not profitable to address; otherwise the for-profit sector would be doing them.

Nonprofit executives assume that effective business methods preclude public good. At the same time, it was generally assumed that business methods were designed to help for-profit companies make as much money as possible by any means possible, which did not necessarily include consideration of the public good. Therefore, the methods themselves were inherently tainted. Most nonprofit executives had little or no familiarity and comfort with concepts like business metrics or return on investment. The result was a continued separation between management and the skills that would enable them to perform those functions well.

Business executives are often puzzled by nonprofit business practices. Likewise, experienced business executives often expressed bafflement at the way nonprofits were managed. Their tendency was to act as if there must be a real but mystifying difference between this field and their for-profit world, or that it was just futile to try to change the status quo. As a result, many board members performed most often (albeit importantly) as a source of a check and a door to other potential supporters. Meanwhile, a lot of important expertise was never put to use, which at times limited the amount of social benefit being provided to the community. While this issue of management is indeed undergoing a time of change, many if not most nonprofit organizations and their boards still tend to operate in the more traditional way today.

Positive organizational image promotes trust and longevity. Lastly, it is still the case that some organizations never seem to change and still do well. Those organizations may appear antiquated, but they survive over time because they successfully establish and keep revitalizing a following of supporters who remain loyal and pass that same commitment on to other family members and friends. The organization's brand usually has evolved to be synonymous with qualities like trust, steadfastness, and the fulfillment of mission. There are not many such groups.

What Is Changing?

To begin, the age of doing good at any cost is coming to a close. Donors are no longer willing or able year after year to support the number of organizations that are appealing for funds at the levels required to provide the services needed to address community issues at the scale at which they now exist. Appeals for support to keep the organizations themselves from collapsing in times of trouble are increasingly less effective. Nonprofit organizations are the means, not the mission.

Nonprofits are expected to think more like businesses. For

> *If you think change is difficult you're going to like irrelevance even less.*
>
> —General Eric Shinseki, U.S. Army Chief of Staff

many, that concept is and will be hard to understand, accept, and implement. But of all the changes taking place, this is the most universal and influential. In his monograph, *Good to Great in the Social Sectors*, Jim Collins points out that differences do, in fact, exist between the sectors, and these differences must be accounted for in management and planning. However, there is little dispute that the increased use of business skills, information, and methods is now important for the success of most nonprofit organizations. Ethics and the problems that arise in their absence are common to every sector.

Nonprofits are beginning to use for-profit business methods. As a result, more nonprofit board members and executives are working on effectively applying business models to improve the performance of nonprofit organizations. Among the results they are producing are an increase in the social benefits they are creating for each donated dollar and the more effective use of resources, including staff and volunteer time. Tom Ralser effectively covers this concept in his book, *ROI for Non-Profits,* and organizations like Social Venture Partners International are providing worldwide management support for these changes in process and outlook.

Donor needs are changing in the new millennium. Another substantial change is that donor needs now are as important as the needs of the organizations they support. A donation today, particularly among younger donors, can be as much an act of self-fulfillment as of community involvement. Organizations that fail to get to know and understand the interests of their individual donors and rely only on repeating a heartfelt appeal about their mission will tend to leave funding on the proverbial table. Greater immediate and long-term support is now more likely when an organization can identify and address a direct link between a donor's personal interests and its own outcomes.

A CASE STUDY: MANAGING CHANGE

An indicative moment of for-profit and nonprofit business thinking coming together took place in a board-level working session of the Access Sacramento public access media organization. The organization was funded by the region's Cable Commission and charged with giving access to the cable media to any member of the community for any topic within very broad guidelines designed to control pornography, hate-mongering, and the like. Anyone could put anything on the air they wanted, and they did.

The problem was that they needed to attract and be recognized as having a larger audience. Meanwhile, the Cable Commission was free to reduce its level of annual support, and they did. In addition, there was no donor base to mobilize, nor any widely acknowledged public benefit that might inspire a group to underwrite an open channel that only a few people were watching. To begin addressing this issue, the organization began by creating its own programming that included coverage of local high school sporting events, community celebrations, awards ceremonies, parades, prominent speakers, and civic forums. This programming was, in fact, attracting viewers.

To explore further options, the organization convened a planning meeting attended by board members, current program producers, and respected former leaders from the local commercial broadcasting industry. The former industry leaders were there because they were interested in the fact that while commercial news reporting was being cut due to financial constraints industry-wide, local independent reporting on the Internet and on channels like community access was on the rise. The access channel was well-positioned to respond to this situation if a financially sustainable model could be identified to support the programming and the channel overall.

After the basic introductions and statements about why each participant saw value in the work of the channel, one member asked for a review of the organization's mission statement. The group judged the mission statement sufficiently inspiring and specific to provide an acceptable basis for getting started. The board members agreed that the statement could be updated as a result of this planning process, if necessary.

One of the representatives from the commercial media industry said that their business development executive once had told them that they were not in the news business but instead were in the "eyeball" business—meaning that their commercial value was based on how many people were watching. Getting people to watch was, therefore, the guide for what they covered and how they covered it. At that point, a community program production team representative said that they had strongly avoided being influenced by such commercial pressures over the years and that their program was, therefore, intrinsically of a different value.

That was a critical moment. It was pointed out that unless the public access channel had a way to get the Cable Commission to reinstate its support, then it too was in the "eyeball business." The channel's value would be assessed according to how effectively they could address the unmet need for information in the community by providing a different point of view than competing commercial stations and attracting, as a result, a larger viewing audience. As with their commercial counterparts, donors and sponsors might then take an interest if more people were watching. At the end of this first meeting, the group had inspired itself to come back very soon to work on a specific plan to carry out the idea. The turning point came when they found a common ground between the nonprofit and the for-profit management models and could start using the skills of both to meet a community need.

William Packard, co-founder of the Hewlett-Packard Corporation, once was asked what cause attracted him the most and what recognition received for a gift to that cause had meant the most to him. He immediately said that education was his top priority and that his most memorable recognition was a group of children from a far-away school that came to his office, sang him a song and sat on his lap telling him stories about the things they were learning. A plaque would not have done it.

Donors are increasingly exhausted and cynical from getting multiple requests not only from the same organizations but also from a cacophony of others that seem to be serving the same purpose with only minor distinctions in the methods. They are asking why more groups are not working together and if indeed so many groups, each with expensive overhead costs, are really necessary.

Donors desire greater connection with the people served. This continuing trend is highlighted by the fact that donor-directed online giving is gaining in popularity. Donors can bypass what they often believe are the unnecessary costs associated with giving to a nonprofit and get the immediate feeling of satisfaction by giving directly to the recipient, like a family in need of money for rent or a teacher in need of classroom supplies. This trend will continue to grow while and until nonprofit groups develop ways to provide those same or greater benefits while still covering their costs.

The donor advisory services profession is a new player. Major banks and investment companies, for example, are among the industries that are starting to offer high-net-worth clients not only advice on income investments but also on making successful social investments. The biggest challenge to the growth and value of this service will be

A CASE STUDY: COMMUNITY IMPACT

The idea of solving social issues rather than simply maintaining them is a new challenge to which very few nonprofits and communities have been ready to respond. But there are some new exceptions. For example, the United Way in Santa Barbara, California, engaged in a potentially very different and very impactful approach to this issue.

A few years ago the leadership and staff of that UW chapter made the important observations that foundations, government agencies and individual donors in their area were giving away a lot of money every year but were rarely working together, and that the problems they were each trying to solve were not changing. So the United Way hosted a series of large community meetings with the various stakeholder groups to discuss an alternative. At the risk of oversimplifying, they posed two core questions:

1. What are the three most urgent issues/problems facing this community?
2. Given the chance to solve each of those problems, would you as donors be willing to pool all of your support together for five years to do so?

The answer to the first question regarding the top issues was: successful children and youth (Santa Barbara reportedly has one of the highest illiteracy rates per capita in the country), independent seniors, and strong families. The answer to the second question was "yes." The participants also recommended that the United Way manage the overall effort because it was capable of doing the job and did not have its own program bias. As that program, which is called Power of Partnership, gets further underway, it holds the possibility of creating a model for actually improving the quality of communities wherever there is the will, money, and organization to do so.

maintaining the satisfaction of clients over time. Will the staff of a bank, for example, have sufficient direct experience with the non-profit sector to know how to help clients reach their personal philanthropic objectives successfully? Setting measurable standards and controlling quality are likely to be important in maintaining the perceived value of this new and growing service.

Metrics provide essential tools for judging value. Another new challenge for nonprofits is in trying to find ways to get donors to use something other than how much out of every donated dollar goes to administra-tive costs to evaluate the effectiveness of a nonprofit program or organization. This is important because, in an effort to cut costs to meet those kinds of objectives, nonprofits run the risk of cutting too far to get donor approval and as a result harming their ability to perform their mission. At the core of this issue is the question of how to judge value in the nonprofit sector. When someone buys a consumer product, for example an iPod, no one knows or cares how much of the cost of that product was spent on administration; the product is valued on its own terms, and the internal costs of creating it are assumed. Nonprofits are in the process of trying to find a new way of valuing their products and services that donors will accept. The solution cannot come too soon.

Partnerships offer benefits. Partnerships between and among non-profits, for-profits, and government are taking place more frequently, but there is still a general hesitancy in each sector to work together, usually because the models for success are not well known. Some nonprofits try to do "everything" related to their cause. For some that can work. For others a better strategy is to do one or a very few things extremely well and partner with other organizations to deliver the balance of the services to the community. While each approach has its pitfalls, collaboration allows the case for each organization to become a little clearer and easier for donors to understand and support, and in some cases, operating costs can also be reduced. As donors become increasingly intolerant of duplicative service and costs and vote with their checkbooks for change, the collaborative partnership approach may be the beginning of a solution.

Corporate partnerships require value propositions. Many corporations have all but eliminated their community giving programs, so nonprofits now have to learn how to develop value propositions in order to partner with the marketing office instead. For example, some organizations are still trying to "sell" sponsorships at their golf tournaments and other events as valuable community visibility opportunities for companies. They will now have to re-package that presentation to show a direct tie-in to the actual business goals and objectives of each company. As a case in point, one corporate sponsor told a nonprofit that it would give the group's golf tournament sponsorship a one-year test. The company wanted to know who would be in each foursome with its sales representatives so that throughout the following year, the sales and marketing staff could track the impact of those new relationships on actual sales. If the results were high enough, the company would invest again in the tournament in the following year. Sometimes from the corporate donor's perspective, it is not philanthropy; it is business.

Public/private partnership can bring the best from both worlds. As national, state, and local public budgets are reduced in the face of economic challenges, more government-related agencies and departments are creating or helping to create nonprofit support organizations that can help carry out public/private partnerships and raise private donations for specific programs or services that neither sector can carry out alone.

A CASE STUDY: PUBLIC/PRIVATE PARTNERSHIP

The Leland Stanford Mansion Foundation was one such nonprofit created by private citizens, many of whom attended Stanford University, to help California State Parks renovate and re-open the historic Leland Stanford Mansion State Park near the capitol. The mansion was the home and office of Governor and Mrs. Leland Stanford and the birthplace of their son and namesake of the university, Leland Stanford Jr. California State Parks had acquired the property, which had deteriorated considerably, but could not afford the immense renovation involved. The foundation raised $11 million in private support and helped secure another $11 million in public funding. It also brought experienced private sector construction and renovation leaders to the project. The mansion now serves as the state's protocol center for receiving visiting dignitaries, as well as a popular public tour venue.

Partnerships like these have some unique limitations as well as some real advantages in terms of fundraising. One of the attractions to donors is the fact that, in many cases, government agencies have enough money to keep the lights on and provide the basic services but not enough to produce real quality of service. Nonprofits spend a lot of time raising money to keep their lights on, which donors hate to pay for. Government agencies are also often very good at providing high-quality service. The implication is that there are untapped opportunities for nonprofits and government agencies to work together for the benefit of the community that again neither can do as well on their own. There are some challenges inherent in such partnerships, but there are also a growing number of examples showing how those can potentially be mitigated.

Social enterprise, social entrepreneurship, and venture philanthropy offer new revenue models. One of the more innovative areas of change in the nonprofit sector is that of social enterprise, social entrepreneurism, and venture philanthropy. J. Gregory Dees, author of *Enterprising Nonprofits*, describes social entrepreneurism like this:

> (Social entrepreneurism) combines the passion of a social mission with an image of business-like discipline, innovation, and determination commonly associated with, for instance, the high-tech pioneers of Silicon Valley. The time is certainly ripe for entrepreneurial approaches to social problems. Many governmental and philanthropic efforts have fallen far short of our expectations. Major social sector institutions are often viewed as inefficient, ineffective, and unresponsive. Social entrepreneurs are needed to develop new models for a new century.

Another description says it like this:

> Social entrepreneurs are individuals with innovative solutions to society's most pressing social problems. They are ambitious and persistent, tackling major social issues and offering new ideas for wide-scale change. Each social entrepreneur presents ideas that are user-friendly, understandable, ethical, and engage widespread support in order to maximize the number of local people

that will stand up, seize their idea, and implement it. In other words, every leading social entrepreneur is a mass recruiter of local changemakers—a role model proving that citizens who channel their passion into action can do almost anything.[1]

Venture philanthropists are donors who approach giving similarly to the way venture capitalists invest in a business. They may support the creation or expansion of a social enterprise, put time and money into building the operational capacity of a nonprofit organization, invest in a social benefit for-profit company, or get involved in any or all of the above.

Social entrepreneurism is not only an approach to developing effective solutions to community issues; it also is becoming a popular field of study and a focus of career development. According to the University of the Pacific, which has a very active international Global Center of Social Enterprise Development on its campus, there currently are 26 universities and colleges in the United States that have Centers for Social Entrepreneurship. Twenty, including Harvard, Yale, Stanford, University of California Berkeley, and Northwestern, have graduate studies programs and three have MBA programs built around this field of study. Similar programs are being created around the world. Students may pursue jobs in the nonprofit sector. Some may work in the for-profit sector but take board positions or otherwise volunteer and be more effective as a result. Some may work in companies and help them adopt effective corporate social responsibility agendas that impact the essential quality of products and services in the marketplace and community.

Social enterprise in the nonprofit sector can range from selling tickets for a theater performance, to running a thrift shop to generate income and provide training for victims of domestic violence, to operating an entirely income-supported bakery or labor service business that trains and employs adults with physical and mental disabilities. PRIDE Industries in Sacramento, Rubicon in San Francisco, and Greysen Industries in New Jersey are but a few of the many, many examples of such social enterprise projects. Many more exist in other countries. India, for example, is particularly active in this part of the field. The social enterprise model is producing more and more examples to address social needs and reduce the burden on philanthropy.

For-profit businesses of all kinds are starting to consider doing some of the work traditionally thought of as the domain of non-profits, and doing it profitably. As more examples come about, they, in turn, are raising the question "If they can do it, why aren't the nonprofits doing it the same way and simply plowing profits back into their programs to lessen the burden on philanthropy?" It is a reasonable question. Indications are that nonprofits can indeed, more often than previously supposed, solve social issues creatively and achieve sustainability based all or in part on an earned-income model rather than the purely donor-driven one.

A CASE STUDY: SOCIAL ENTERPRISE

One example of how a project can be transformed by social enterprise took place with a newly formed environmental organization called Discover the Delta in California. The founder and visionary for that organization created a plan for a major education center. He wanted to raise $2 million in major donations to build it. However, he had not built a base of major donor prospects and the chances of doing so quickly were slim.

Meanwhile, on the land adjacent to the parcel being purchased for the center was a brand-new building designed specifically for use as a farmers market. Both contiguous parcels were located on the corner of two of the busiest roadways in the region. The second parcel and building where the farmers market stood could be acquired. The business research showed that a well-managed farmers market could conservatively produce sufficient income to support itself and the education center's projected annual operating budget. So instead of a fundraising plan, a business plan was created for the center and an integrated farmers market. The combined center and farmers market featured the agricultural products of and information about the local area, which tied comfortably to the educational mission.

When the plan was reviewed by the board, one member stood and said that he now could see how the project could be successful, and he was, therefore, willing to co-sign on a bank note to buy the land and prepare for construction. Others in the community also stepped up to co-sign the notes. With that support in hand, the group met with major donor prospects who were very willing to discuss the project based on the planning and investment that was already involved.

As this phenomenon continues to take hold, it is likely that the issue of for-profit groups asking why their nonprofit competitors get tax breaks will resurface. One response, of course, will be that nonprofits do not have the ability to put their excess earnings into the pockets of the investors, board, or staff and that tax relief balances that lack of financial incentive. In the end, when there are competing products and services in both sectors, one proposal will be to let the marketplace decide which represents the best value and most trustworthy brand.

A *"Fourth Sector"—the for-benefit sector—is emerging.* Lastly, there are a few other new management options in the community service landscape. One is the Fourth Sector. Around the world, entrepreneurial social sector leaders and problem solvers are blending the attributes of the private sector, public sector, and nonprofit sector to create new solutions to existing social problems. Ignoring the boundaries of each sector allows these new planners to tap into their strengths and eliminate the weaknesses to produce more widely applicable organizational solutions. A working definition provided by the Green House glossary is: "The Fourth Sector model is sometimes referred to as a For-Benefit organization, and the sector itself is also referred to as the For-Benefit Sector. . . . For-Benefits are a new class of organization. They are driven by a social purpose; they are economically self-sustaining; and they seek to be socially, ethically, and environmentally responsible."

Another new option is the proposed B Corporation. A working definition for that concept is: B corporations (the B standing for "beneficial") are a type of organization proposed by B Lab of Pennsylvania. They use the power of business to create public benefit, with three criteria. B Corporations:

1. Meet comprehensive and transparent social and environmental performance standards.
2. Legally expand the responsibilities of the corporation to include stakeholder interests.
3. Build collective voice through the power of the unifying B Corporation brand.

There is no telling where options like these will take social activism and community service problem-solving, but they are currently part of a growing mix of options and opportunities that, to greater or lesser degrees, will have an impact on the nonprofit sector in how it is operated, funded, and evaluated.

Tax law may impact nonprofits in unpredictable ways. A final factor that may impose change on the nonprofit sector is adjustments in the tax law to reduce the amounts that can be deducted for donations by select classes of taxpayers. It is unclear what, if any, impact such changes will have on philanthropy. Tax incentives to date have not appeared to have played a significant role in donors' decisions to give. However, planned giving, which often is designed to maximize those benefits for a donor, may be affected, or not.

Conclusion

Is there a future for nonprofits? In light of all these changes, the nonprofit groups that may have the best chance of success are those that can select and act on those factors that can or will impact them. New organizations have the advantage of not being burdened with traditional ways of operating and can develop a management approach and method of service delivery that produces the greatest benefits for the least amount of resources. Established groups have the advantage of being just that—established, known, and trusted. Making changes may be harder from an ingrained habit standpoint, but supporters will be more prone to go along with changes when they come from a trusted and familiar source.

The future of nonprofit organizations does not seem in any way to be in jeopardy. Indeed, the need for nonprofit services will likely grow. It is predicted, for example, that changes in the environment will cause large migrations of people and animals to new locations, causing the need for major social service support. New innovations in medicine, education, environmental management, and much more also will bring about changes in the needs and wants of many people in communities worldwide.

However, some individual organizations will risk disappearing unless they prove they are filling a real and important need and are not duplicating the work of other peer organizations. Others will risk becoming comparatively irrelevant if they do not maintain a leadership role in how effectively they carry out their missions.

Individual donors and volunteers will for the foreseeable future continue to want to get involved, give back, and make a difference. More companies are likely to want to be socially responsible as part of increasing their own business base and being recognized as valuable members of the community. Governments will find it harder to deliver the quality of service their constituents need and want and will work more with nonprofits to help with, and in some cases, take over select community services.

It is important then that nonprofit managers and supporters learn to adapt to and take advantage of the changes that have been and are continuing to impact this sector. There are methods available to help guide those efforts, and board members with business experience can be an ongoing source of that information and knowledge. Nonprofit leaders who are open and responsive to change will find themselves faced with nearly unlimited opportunities and challenges.

CHAPTER 4

High-Impact Nonprofit-Corporate Partnerships

EUGENIA V. COLÓN

Over the past 40 years, the U.S. economy has experienced six recessions that have lasted 10.7 months on average. Although the end of the 2008–2009 recession is much discussed, the most skeptical economists believe the magnitude of this recession could be the most severe in decades. The gravity of the economic downturn is driving sweeping change in the public sector as well as in the marketplace. Nonprofits and corporations alike are struggling to survive the disappearance of wealth from capital markets and the resulting reductions in their budgets and staff.

> *Life's most persistent and urgent question is: What are you doing for others?*
>
> —Dr. Martin Luther King, Jr.

While philanthropy has become a critical component of corporate citizenship that is deeply embedded throughout a company's operations, in the current climate, issues related to the economic downturn dominate the concerns of corporate giving officers[1]. In a 2009 survey of philanthropic drivers, the shift toward more critical business issues and an increased emphasis on measuring giving outcomes is reflected in the factors identified by corporate giving officers as primary considerations. These primary factors include limits on budgetary resources (56 percent); the current economic downturn in general (50 percent); and aligning more closely with business needs (47 percent).[2] Like their corporate counterparts, nonprofit leaders are equally focused on developing and leveraging strategies for sustainability and growth in an environment marked by drastically reduced funding.

While estimates as to the duration of the recession vary, perhaps the most critical economic projection is that recovery is likely to be gradual rather than a robust turnaround in economic activity.[3] Daunting as this may seem, embedded in every problem is a solution waiting to be grasped; and the current economic crisis is no exception. Adversity forces us out of our comfort zones, requiring that we deconstruct and reformulate our approaches to the world. In the current environment, nonprofits have a rare opportunity to position themselves and their sector for long-term sustainability through a revitalized approach to corporations, an approach that more deeply engages corporations and tactically concentrates on shared needs, goals, and capacity to increase social impact through more pragmatic, intentionally designed collaborative efforts.

A deliberate move by nonprofits toward more dynamic, comprehensive, and results-driven corporate partnerships aimed at achieving systemic change can bring extraordinary power to solving complex social problems. In this prolonged recession, the nonprofit sector's approach to corporate funders has the potential to reshape the nonprofit sector—and corporate philanthropy—in positive ways that will endure long beyond the current economic crisis.

Trends in Corporate Giving

Corporate America has been hard hit by the economic recession that began in 2007, particularly the banking and finance sectors that have been the source of approximately 25 percent of corporate foundation giving in recent years. However, the effects of this economic debacle extend well beyond banking and finance, affecting corporate earnings and philanthropic budgets across the board.

Throughout the United States and around the globe, corporations are reassessing the needs of the charitable marketplace, adapting by setting new philanthropic priorities

> *When fate hands you a lemon, make lemonade.*
>
> —Dale Carnegie

for their programs to better reflect and respond to identified needs, and reallocating philanthropic resources accordingly.[4] Many corporations have scaled back or suspended charitable giving including traditional corporate sponsorships, grants, and other direct support that nonprofits have come to rely upon. The economy has forced corporations to target philanthropic funding to fewer priorities and to concentrate on ensuring that these charitable investments produce measurable results. According to the annual forecasting survey conducted by the Foundation Center, 51 percent of corporate foundations expected to decrease giving in 2009, and more than three-quarters of these funders anticipated decreases in giving of greater than 10 percent. Yet, despite the decline in corporate profits reported by 68 percent of respondents to a June 2009 Conference Board survey, 53 percent of these same respondents actually *increased* their giving, with 27 percent reporting an increase of 10 percent or more.[5] The area of the largest predicted growth for 2009 was the non-cash expenditure of volunteer and pro bono support, reported by 45 percent of respondents.[6] The biggest cut in funding was projected to be in the area of event sponsorship, with resources falling for 55 percent of survey respondents.[7]

Of even greater significance for nonprofits are three predominant trends in corporate philanthropy that have emerged in this recession and are reinventing corporate philanthropy. These trends are: (1) a growing focus on long-term, systemic solutions to critical social problems; (2) innovative approaches to partnerships to increase the leverage and impact of contributions; and (3) doing more to respond to the direct impact of the economy on people's basic needs.[8] More than eight in ten corporations are encouraging more volunteerism among their employees; roughly 15 percent of corporate funders plan to increase in-kind donations, including skill-based services; and 12 percent plan to increase product donations.[9]

Moreover, the tendency to be more responsive to people's basic needs is reflected in data showing the number of U.S. corporate funders providing crisis-related funding more than doubled as housing and shelter, including foreclosure prevention, received the lion's share of corporate dollars. Emergency assistance, including food assistance, received the second largest share of dollars, and it garnered the greatest share in number of commitments.[10]

These prevailing trends represent a corporate philanthropy that is becoming ever more strategic and intensely collaborative in response not only to funding constraints but with the ultimate goal of achieving greater, more enduring impact. Corporations are focusing on specific priorities, aligning philanthropic and business goals, and measuring the return on charitable investments. They are requiring greater accountability from grantees with an emphasis on measurable outcomes. Systemic change funding is the path being taken by the majority of major corporate philanthropists who seek to work through multiple channels and with numerous partners, with the goal of eradicating substantial problems. This corporate focus on social projects capable of achieving systemic change is consistent with the concurrent nonprofit approach for dealing with society's most intractable problems.

But the most striking movement prompted by the need to accomplish more with less is toward greater collaboration— between and among corporations themselves as well as across sectors. More and more corporate funders are taking part in collegial networks to exchange ideas and best practices, funding partnerships, and sharing administrative support staff and functions. A sampling of 2009 grants and activities illustrates what amounts to a strategic shift in corporate philanthropy to a more intensely cooperative, socially responsive undertaking:

- State Street Corp. in Boston is spearheading a funders' learning collaborative that has generated interest from a broad range of funders who have formed working groups to study and address youth violence in Boston's highest-risk neighborhoods.
- The Walmart Foundation donated nearly $8 million to support summer feeding programs for children most at risk of hunger

and to provide resources for food banks throughout the United States.

• Boston Scientific Corporation has focused its national grant-making on reducing health disparities for underserved populations, including the homeless and migrant farm workers and their families, and GE gave $20 million to address the needs of the homeless.

Undoubtedly, the ongoing economic crisis is driving a new era in corporate philanthropy characterized by greater reflection and evaluation coupled with the determination to achieve greater positive social impact despite reduced resources. Toward the same end, nonprofit leaders are currently engaged in much the same process of critical assessment and deliberation. Closer collaboration between nonprofit organizations and corporations founded on the challenges, core values, and goals they share will increase their capacity, collectively and individually, to meet myriad social challenges whether in a boom or bust economy.

Areas of Corporate Funding Interest

Over the past 20 years, the nonprofit sector in the United States has swelled to immense proportions. Today the sector comprises an estimated 1.5 million organizations, has total annual income of approximately $1 trillion, and employs 10 percent of the American workforce. In short, the nonprofit sector is a massive economic driver. Yet despite the unequivocal value of the nonprofit sector, the economic downturn is compelling many nonprofits to reevaluate their missions, strategic priorities, relationships, and, for some, their very existence. Throughout the sector, financial cutbacks are forcing organizations to assess long-term sustainability, restructure programs and staffing, explore new revenue streams, and seek non-traditional partnerships such as formal mergers.

In these times of great need and diminished resources, many nonprofits are embracing the inevitability of change by re-evaluating their efforts overall, and cross-sector partnerships in particular. The recession may be cutting into fundraising results, but nonprofit

> *It is better to light a candle than curse the darkness.*
>
> —Eleanor Roosevelt

leaders are proactively focused on strategic planning, measuring results, working smarter, and forging capacity-building relationships. Recognizing the value of effective business strategies, they are looking to appropriately adapt best corporate practices including exploring social enterprise opportunities and entrepreneurial approaches; incorporating business techniques that build on their core competencies; and purposefully changing their service models.

Among the consequences of the economic crisis is a public hue and cry for increased accountability and transparency from public and private sector organizations alike. Nonprofits should more actively engage and involve corporations in creating the conditions and providing the resources necessary for nonprofits to meet these demands. To do so will enable growth and foster the relationships required for long-term sustainability. Surviving economic downturns and being in a position to take full advantage of boom periods will require nonprofits to adopt a more business-like operations model with the aim of becoming high-performance organizations fueled by learning cultures, driven by continuous improvement, and sustained by high-quality, demonstrable results.

Traditionally, corporate philanthropy has been strategically focused on building community support, public image, brand awareness, and consumer allegiance through providing primarily financial charitable support. However, the definition of a socially responsible company is evolving from a transactional approach—providing financial support—to a transformational approach involving the full range of corporate resources, talents, and funding to enable nonprofit organizations to achieve their goals more effectively. In 2008, the greatest surge in corporate philanthropic giving was in non-cash contributions, which rose nearly 35 percent among those companies whose giving increased.[11] More and more corporations are coming to appreciate the benefits of "transformational investing"—giving time as well as money—that enables a company to do good while creating positive brand experiences both internally and externally.[12]

Leveraging Convergence

The dynamic environment created by the current recession is rife with challenges, but it has also opened up new opportunities for nonprofit success. The time is ripe to expand the definitions of nonprofit-corporate partnerships and, thereby, of corporate philanthropy. What follows is a discussion of contemporary areas of corporate philanthropic interests and approaches to developing cross-sector partnerships that leverage the convergence of shared goals and complementary interests.

Collaboration   No strategy has been more emphatically propounded by corporations and nonprofits alike than the need to forge new partnerships. Nonprofits should seek to frame partnerships with corporations in ways that take into account not only the nonprofit's needs and goals, but equally considers and appropriately addresses a company's core business, community development, customer relations, branding, and public image goals with an emphasis on public relations.

Corporations today are motivated by a sense of urgency reflected in the heightened shift toward collaboration among themselves. They are choosing to use the economic crisis as an opportunity to come together to create transformational change in the business sector including in the area of corporate philanthropy. They are seeking increased interaction, challenging each other, and sharing ideas and resources. Around the globe corporations are setting up funders' collaboratives and partnerships that allow for work on a larger scale and also increase visibility, the sharing of risk, and the ability to leverage dollars. But arguably the greatest value participants attribute to these collaboratives are the deepened relationships with other funders, leading to even broader partnerships and greater social impact. Cross-sector collaborations enjoy these benefits as well, particularly when nonprofits involve corporations as genuine partners. Finding more ways to collaborate is a strategic imperative for these times and will continue to be for the foreseeable future. Nonprofits should pursue opportunities for joint planning and coordination with corporate funders, creating an environment that welcomes advice and input from both parties, as well as from the communities they serve. Nonprofits should regard business as an ally, welcoming its immense capacity to contribute to solving complex social problems. On critical social issues where companies have reason to be involved, substantially greater progress can be made if nonprofits can find effective ways of engaging companies in cross-sector partnerships. In adopting a more positive perception of corporate involvement, nonprofits can tap into a wealth of resources that have long been beyond their reach.

Deep engagement allows nonprofits the opportunity to take the lead in defining and communicating to corporate funders the nonprofit sector's value and strengths, limitations and needs, toward building the sector's overall capacity to achieve the positive systemic social change that is the shared aim of funders and nonprofits. For example, there is a growing sense among nonprofit organizations that there is a need for a system-wide assessment to address questions of duplication of efforts, proliferation of nonprofits, financial stability, and sustainability. The current economic climate is inducing a growing number of nonprofits to consider the value of intra-sector collaboration. They are exploring opportunities to work together to achieve operational efficiencies such as joint services, shared databases, consolidation of backroom operations, and professional development for nonprofit staff. In considering such joint ventures, some organizations are entertaining the possibility of more permanent strategic alliances with other nonprofits such as mergers. Yet, many are at a loss as to how best to move from collaboration as a concept or occasional joint project to a routine business practice.

Nonprofits should look to the expertise and experience of corporate partners to achieve the best possible outcomes and work together with corporate partners to explore a wide range of collaborative options. A possible approach is using professional firms, on a pro bono basis, to conduct feasibility studies on when and where collaboration could work, especially for mergers and consolidations. In the process, nonprofits are likely to enjoy the added benefits of increased involvement and commitment of corporate partners and, ultimately, greater likelihood of financial support.

In developing these more involved relationships, nonprofit leaders should meet with corporate funders to discuss the top three business issues outlined in their nonprofit's strategic plan for the purpose of inviting funders to identify expertise within their organizations to help address the nonprofit's operational needs. Nonprofit organizations should make a point of teaming up with corporations that address similar issues or work in an industry that can actively develop or provide solutions to problems that are at the heart of the nonprofit's mission, for instance, food scarcity, clean water, heart disease, or homelessness.

Although companies exist to generate profits, they often have far greater ability to lead social progress than they are currently invited to exercise. Maximizing a corporation's full potential to develop and implement solutions not only offers more powerful benefits to society but enables companies to distinguish themselves and earn reputations for corporate responsibility that can enhance their brands, motivate their employees, and strengthen their licenses to operate.[13] It is important to note that, in a recent survey of corporate funders, 48 percent cited brand visibility as increasing in importance, and the relationship of corporate philanthropy to broader corporate sustainability goals was cited by 46 percent.[14] Therefore, in cultivating and soliciting corporate support, nonprofits should be prepared to emphasize the value of co-branding and the ways in which a comprehensive partnership can increase public approval and attract greater support and customer loyalty.

Many companies are looking for ways to demonstrate their corporate responsibility by developing affirmative approaches to solving social problems, but they often lack a full understanding of the issues and so cannot frame realistic goals. Nonprofits often have a deeper understanding of the problem, which enables them to help companies devise more comprehensive strategies and to set more ambitious, yet attainable, goals. In closer collaborations, nonprofits should involve corporate donors and prospects in ongoing dialogue to discuss challenges and develop creative strategies for addressing problems, while building trust with key audiences within and across sectors.

Planning Nonprofits should work with corporate funders to develop a clearly defined engagement and partnership plan that addresses ways in which comprehensive corporate support (including pro bono, in-kind, and cash contributions) will contribute to the strength and sustainability of the nonprofit; achieve measurable, high-impact results; and increase a corporation's value and positive response to its brand.

The planning process might include taking advantage of corporate expertise to develop new revenue streams such as earned income. Corporations typically conduct competitive market analyses and feasibility studies to assess product viability and consumer interest. Instead of paying a marketing consultant to perform these services, nonprofits should look to corporate partners to provide such services on a pro bono basis, thereby releasing valuable nonprofit funds for critical direct services or operating costs, which otherwise would have been paid to a consultant. Additionally, because these planning processes involve a high level of engagement, they inevitably result in forging deeper bonds, commitment, and buy-in among and between all parties resulting, ultimately, in more enduring, productive relationships.

Pro Bono Services and Volunteerism   The historic signing in 2009 of the Serve America Act has prompted serious reflection among corporations as to the role the business community can and should play in answering the call to service in the coming months and years. The Serve America Act is proving to be an important driver of increased corporate volunteerism, with 44 percent of corporate grantmakers indicating their companies would increase resources for volunteerism in direct response to the national call for service.[15] The renewed spirit of civic engagement in corporate America makes this an ideal time for nonprofits to design highly intentional partnership proposals to corporations. They should include specific plans for using corporate pro bono expertise in pragmatic ways geared toward building nonprofit capacity and contributing to its long-term sustainability.

Nonprofit organizations must expand their thinking beyond cash support and recognize pro bono support as a currency that can produce considerable benefits that will strengthen and ensure organizational viability. The pro bono support will also cement enduring relationships with corporate partners through a necessarily deeper level of engagement. With philanthropic dollars increasingly scarce, the need to hasten the adoption of pro bono support as a complementary giving strategy has never been more critical. Corporate pro bono services offer creative, cost-effective means by which businesses and nonprofits can offset declines in corporate giving to maintain, or even increase, their impact on the communities they serve.

Many nonprofits have difficulty understanding or envisioning the full complement of resources a corporation can bring to bear on solving a social problem. To increase mutual understanding, nonprofits and corporations should routinely conduct quarterly meetings to discuss and identify capabilities and needs, and to develop and review multi-year partnership plans that encompass pro bono and in-kind support, as well as cash contributions. In taking such a long-term approach to corporate giving, nonprofit organizations should look to corporations to provide the pro bono and in-kind tactical support required to fulfill critical functions such as developing communications plans, feasibility studies, strategic plans, operational and financial audits, and public relations campaigns.[16] Pro bono and skill-based volunteerism are rapidly emerging as a valuable form of currency, an opportunity to fully maximize corporate assets, especially when demand for nonprofit services are on the rise and corporate giving is on the decline.[17] Corporate contributions of skill-based services represent critical support for nonprofits, many of which cannot afford to pay for consultants. Nonprofits and corporations today have a unique opportunity and national "charge" to think creatively about how to capitalize on the growing market for pro bono services not simply during economic downturns, but in ways that will strengthen nonprofits and maximize corporate resources and philanthropic impact in any climate.[18]

Accountability and Measurement Nationwide, there is increased demand for organizations—both corporate and nonprofit—to be more accountable and to provide evidence of performance results. If they intend to be sustainable in the long term, it is imperative that nonprofits demonstrate quantifiable impact on a social problem and show as precisely as possible how corporate support will increase impact. The principal management issue of increasing importance to corporate funders is measurement of outcomes.

However, the trend toward an ever-growing interdependency between the business and nonprofit sectors holds great promise for building the public trust that transparency and accountability will bring to both. Given the demand for greater accountability and measurement, and the nonprofit sector's lack of expertise in the sophisticated practices essential to meeting these demands, nonprofits and corporate partners should work together to develop the metrics that will provide clear accounts of the breadth and depth of a nonprofit's social impact. Corporations expert in consumer and market analysis, benchmarking, and survey metrics can provide these professional services on a pro bono basis. In the process, nonprofit organizations can help corporations to better understand the social repercussions of their work and to refine their approaches to social responsibility.[19]

Marketing and Communications Plans As nonprofits struggle to do more work with fewer resources, many consider outsourcing back-office functions such as accounting and human-resources management. Many nonprofits say financial planning, finding and retaining qualified staff, and communications are areas in which they need help; but they agree the most pressing need is to improve marketing and communications plans, including publications and materials. There is consensus among nonprofits that improved communications and marketing plans—including social marketing that uses various media markets and technology—are essential to boosting investments in the nonprofit sector. Yet, by and large, nonprofits lack the resources and skills required to develop cutting edge marketing and communications campaigns and tools, particularly in the area of social media—and the costs of outsourcing these functions can be prohibitive for the average nonprofit organization.[20] Nonprofits should look to corporate partners to provide professional support and resources on a pro bono and in-kind basis, in addition to making financial investments in new communications strategies and technologies. In the process of co-designing messages and testing communications and marketing approaches, corporations will gain greater knowledge and appreciation of a nonprofit's value proposition, and nonprofits will learn and internalize skills and techniques that allow them to extend engagement, support, and impact.

Capacity Building More and more companies are looking to support capacity building and to provide operating funds to ensure that nonprofit partners are viable and efficient. For example, in 2009, Bank of America allocated approximately 25 percent of its giving for capacity-building and operating support, and the Boston Foundation unveiled major changes in its grantmaking strategy, announcing "the most dramatic change is a shift of emphasis to unrestricted operating support."[21]

Capacity building provides an ideal channel for soliciting corporate pro bono support in the form of professional services. Such support relieves overburdened nonprofit staff who are often forced to perform functions outside their job description; reduces burnout and turnover; achieves cost savings; and improves overall operations, performance, and impact.

High-Impact Partnerships: Investing for the Upturn

Although the challenges we face are complex, our global society will pay dearly if we do not accelerate our efforts to strategically address pressing needs. Nonprofit organizations and corporations must work together creatively to take full advantage of the positive contributions they can make through public-private partnerships that leverage the full range of their wealth of creativity, resources, expertise, and shared commitment to results. In collaboration with companies, nonprofit leaders should leverage the convergence of the economic climate, national service goals, and corporate transformational investing to develop partnership plans that take advantage of valuable corporate pro bono and volunteer services, strengthen nonprofits' infrastructure and

Coming together is a beginning. Keeping together is progress. Working together is success.

—Henry Ford

operations, respond to companies' branding and public relations' goals—all ultimately working to increase the common good.

High-Impact Models

There is a growing inclination among all funders, but particularly among corporations, to think in fresh ways about corporate social responsibility and corporate philanthropy. They are particularly drawn toward more long-term strategic partnerships involving fewer, longer, more flexible grants that are designed to achieve greater impact. Corporations are also exploring different nonprofit business models to better support meaningful change.[22]

Given their first-hand knowledge of and experience in dealing with difficult social problems, nonprofits should proactively approach corporations to design and implement high-impact models for cross-sector partnerships that integrate pro bono and in-kind support and volunteerism with strategic corporate financial investments. These model partnerships can then be replicated by other corporations and nonprofits nationally and globally.[23]

As a rule, but specifically during economic downturns, partners should consider piloting or building and implementing a piece of a program, positioning it to grow as the economy rebounds and companies begin to see new growth. Over the long term, if nonprofits with corporate partners can create effective models, particularly in economically challenging times, they will have laid the foundation for the sustainability both sectors are aiming for.

There are a number of high-impact models of cross-sector collaboration that nonprofits might look to as they work to develop more productive, enduring relationships with corporations, and a number of these models are briefly discussed below. Nonprofits should think in terms of creating opportunities to make their case to such funder and cross-sector collaboratives as part of routine outreach and cultivation of corporate partners.

The Clinton Global Initiative: Chief among today's high-impact public-private philanthropic models is the Clinton Global Initiative (CGI) which facilitates cross-sector partnerships that create and carry out projects of their own choosing. The CGI community is composed of corporate and nonprofit executives, among others, who work together to develop unique solutions to some of the world's most pressing challenges. Through a unique feature called Commitments to Action, CGI members translate practical goals into meaningful, measurable results. Throughout the year, the CGI functions as a diverse community of change makers who work to develop commitments that are consistent with members' core philanthropic and business goals.

CGI commitments typically involve diverse partnerships across sectors with members combining efforts to expand the impact of ideas. In 2009, recognizing that "global businesses are uniquely positioned to harness the power of intellectual and financial capital to create progress," the CGI targeted four Action Areas to engage business in addressing global challenges. These Action Areas reflect an approach to business that should be instructive to nonprofits: Harnessing Innovation for Development, Strengthening Infrastructure, Developing Human Capital, and Financing a Sustainable Future.[24]

The Committee Encouraging Corporate Philanthropy (CECP) is the only international forum of business CEOs and chairpersons focused exclusively on corporate philanthropy. CECP's mission is to lead the business community in raising the level and quality of corporate philanthropy. CECP believes that discipline applies to philanthropy, like any other business function. When companies demonstrate programmatic effectiveness, fiscal accountability, and good stewardship in their philanthropic programs, society and business both stand to benefit greatly. Through innovative philanthropic programs, companies can also improve employee retention and heighten brand recognition.[25]

The Conference Board creates and disseminates knowledge about management and the marketplace to help businesses strengthen their performance and better serve society. The

Conference Board operates as a global independent membership organization working in the public interest. It publishes information and analyses, makes economics-based forecasts and assesses trends, and facilitates learning by creating dynamic communities of interest that bring together senior executives from around the world. The Contributions Council of the Conference Board provides leadership to advance the practice of corporate philanthropy and to underscore its importance to corporations and society by educating council members, other practitioners, and target audiences; identifying key issues; making recommendations to The Conference Board on appropriate areas of research, providing regular opportunities for the exchange of information with council members and with other councils or external groups.[26]

The Philanthropic Initiative, Inc. (TPI) is a nonprofit advisory team that designs, carries out, and evaluates philanthropic programs for individual donors, families, foundations, and corporations. Since inception, TPI's goal has been to help clients to invest in their own values, communities, and societies for maximum impact. TPI also encourages a positive climate for philanthropy and actively promotes effective giving through its work with community foundations, Regional Associations of Grantmakers, and others. TPI's programmatic work includes effective models and promising approaches, design of creative philanthropic strategies that target specific needs and opportunities to make a difference, and implementation and evaluation of these strategies.[27]

The Forum of Regional Associations of Grantmakers is a national philanthropic leader and a network of 33 regional associations of grantmakers. The Forum organizes its activities and applies its resources against six priorities including developing partnerships based on beneficial exchange.[28]

The Alliance for Effective Social Investing is an international effort to identify promising new metrics of organizations' social impact and to promote the development of a more robust environment for effective social investing, replacing financial measures as the sole barometer of an organization's performance.[29]

Remember the Basics

Despite the changing philanthropic and economic landscapes, nonprofits must always keep sight of the fundraising basics that remain among the hallmarks of healthy nonprofit organizations:

- Ensuring that mission, program, and budget are aligned.
- Having diverse revenue streams and offering a variety of ways to give.
- Maintaining a pronounced focus on development activities, particularly outreach and donor relations activities that concentrate on keeping donors and partners involved in ways that work to deepen relationships and strengthen understanding of the case for support.
- Ensuring strong management and a highly engaged team led by board members who are actively participating in fundraising and prospect cultivation.
- Conducting ongoing prospect and donor research that enables effective messages that match a donor's interests and capacity with a nonprofit's goals. It is *always* a perfect time for development officers or research staff to update prospect profiles *before* meetings or calls. Indeed, in today's intensely competitive fundraising climate, it is more important than ever. Knowing more about a prospect's or donor's situation will better prepare a nonprofit to respond to their concerns, interests, and goals.

Conclusion

In this new millennium, we must recognize that our task is not to resist change but to embrace and shape it. Today we are at a breakthrough moment in which nonprofits and corporations can launch a

Never doubt that a small group of thoughtful, committed people can change the world. Indeed, it is the only thing that ever has.

—Margaret Mead

new era of philanthropic collaboration to radiate creative ideas, programs, and practical solutions to the four corners of the world. Together, nonprofits and corporations can determine how best to convert corporate citizenship and nonprofit sustainability into sources of real social and business value through cross-sector partnerships that leverage diverse talent, *all* available resources, and the shared commitment to real results.

CHAPTER 5

Casting Your Net into the Social Media Ocean

PAUL GHIZ

Microblogs, wikis, social networks, video sharing—the list goes on and on. Put another way, Twitter®, Wikipedia®, Facebook®, YouTube®, and the list goes on and on. The social media world is growing at an exponential rate, and you may wonder how your organization can benefit from this phenomenon. What's the value, and how will it help deliver your mission? Perhaps you are simply looking for the answer to the question "Is social media right for us?" Maybe you just love this fast growth space, have dipped your toe in the water, and are ready to put more investment into it, but are not quite sure how to scale your program.

I've been creating and executing Web strategies for nonprofit organizations for almost 15 years and never has there been a forum as open, inexpensive and powerful as the social media world. My clients have experienced significant increases in participation, visibility, and giving through this new outlet. If planned and leveraged properly, your social media strategy can lead your organization to new heights. This chapter will reveal how you may incorporate social media into your institutional advancement strategy, as well as offering tactical advice to raising awareness, empowering constituents, and building your donor base.

What Is Social Media?

Social media and Web 2.0 technologies, or as some refer to it collectively as "the social Web," are an interesting and exciting mash-up of online neighborhoods, transparent user-generated content, opinions, answers, support, and free services. The true jewels of social media are the conversations, not the technology that facilitates the discussion. According to a current Wikipedia entry (9/27/09), "Social media are media designed to be disseminated through social interactions, created using highly accessible and scalable publishing techniques. Social media supports the human need for social interaction, using Internet and Web-based technologies to transform broadcast media monologues (one to many) into social media dialogues (many to many). It supports the democratization of knowledge and information, transforming people from content consumers to content producers." This very transformation of broadcast media into a dialogue is an integral factor as to why social media has exploded in popularity and can be very beneficial to your organization.

I believe the social media world is also a movement, leveraging the power of the people and community where users get to choose, listen, and participate. It aims to enhance creativity, information sharing, and, most notably, collaboration among users. Web 2.0 social media applications take on many shapes and sizes and fall into the following categories:

- Communication (blogs, social networks, news aggregation)
- Collaboration (wikis, social book marking)
- Multimedia (photo sharing, video sharing)
- Entertainment

Social Media by the Numbers

People, of course, are the driving force behind social media. In fact, according to Forrester, *The Growth of Social Technology Adoption 2008*, three out of four Americans are using social technology. Visiting social sites is now the fourth most popular online activity (ahead of personal e-mail) based on Nielsen's recent 2009 study, *Global Faces & Networked Places*. The same study states that 10 percent of all Internet time is spent on social networks.

Now let's take a look at recent metrics from some popular social spots. Did you know that 13 billion articles are now available on Wikipedia.org? Over three and one half billion photos have been archived by Flickr®, and three million tweets is the average daily usage on Twitter. Ever wonder where time goes? There are five billion minutes spent on Facebook and 100 million YouTube videos viewed each day. To some people, this virtual ocean of people interacting is a waste of time, but it does have its advantages. For instance, it played an integral part in the 2008 Presidential election race. Each candidate embraced the social Web to reach unprecedented achievements related to mobilizing supporters and fundraising. But it took planning, faith in social technology, and committed people to break prior barriers and mobilize record numbers of volunteers and voters through social media.

Where do nonprofits stand in the adoption of social technology? These were large, well-funded presidential campaigns; do their experiences stand as models for other nonprofits? *Dartmouth Center for Marketing Research* recently announced that nonprofit organizations have been outpacing corporations in their adoption of social media, with 89 percent of charitable organizations using some form of social media. It makes sense to me, given that nonprofit survival can depend on personal relationships. Nonprofits are using various social outposts to find new messengers with new circles of influence to champion a cause.

Further, the social Web is not just for capturing new donors or mobilizing volunteers. It is also becoming an invaluable arena for sound-boarding new ideas and receiving instantaneous feedback, a popular exercise called crowdsourcing. Obtaining prompt, authentic, and unplugged input from your network can uncover some of the most effective solutions to the challenges you face.

Good intentions do not ensure effective use of social media. For any organization, successful use of new technology requires an overarching strategy to guide the process.

Planning Your Social Media Strategy

Jumping into the social media game requires giving up some editorial control and investing time to learn the tools. Your best chance of success is to integrate social media in your overriding development and marketing strategy. Here are five guidelines to consider when planning your social media strategy:

1. *Discover, Listen, and Learn*—Before crafting a social media plan, learn how to use the various tools in order to have a better understanding of how your organization can benefit. Research and find where your constituency is congregating. Join the community and simply listen to what people are saying. It will open your eyes and turn you into a better social media communicator. Document your findings and share with your team.

2. *Participate, Contribute, and Reciprocate*—Begin engaging in discussions on the different communities. If you add value, your visibility will increase and your network will grow. The more productively you contribute to the conversation, the more likely you will have success engaging them in a new conversation. Certainly your engagement must begin with careful thought about the messages and objectives for each community, but the process of communication is evolutionary. Asking for various types of support from your network will help you better understand where their interests fall. Reciprocating support, feedback, or endorsements will likely enhance your social media position.

3. *Define Goal(s) and Channels*—Start by stating your goal(s) and objectives and how you will measure them. Your goal may be to build your network of friends, also known as friendraising. It may be to recruit volunteers or to acquire new donors. Maybe you want to grow your Web site traffic. You will have to decide which social media tools you will support in order to have the most meaningful conversations.

4. *Develop a Content and Task Plan*—What tactics will be used in your strategy? These questions must be answered up front as

---

you develop your message and make decisions regarding the type of interactions you seek. You will need to develop a task list for each channel and allocate staff to each task. Set a recurring meeting to discuss your efforts, findings, issues, and new ideas. This collaboration will help keep everyone on the same page, foster innovation, and provide a level of accountability.

5. *Analyze and Refine*—Set up reports to track the metrics you have defined, recognizing that some metrics will be more rigid than others. Review your progress as a team and keep your colleagues outside the social media group apprised. You may have master reports for your team and summary reports for others. The knowledge gained from the data collected will likely force adjustments to your media campaign and that's okay. It is a living, breathing forum that requires perpetual refinement.

Having a holistic game plan prior to executing your social media campaign will not only pay off in time savings but will ensure that you reach your goals.

Social Media Tips to Consider

During the past couple of years, I've had the good fortune to plan and drive social media strategies for clients. Along the way, I've compiled several best practices when gearing up to execute the plan.

- First, find natural supporters who are already connected online (influencers) and are having conversations about an issue. Engage them to help. Arm your most ardent ambassadors with information to amplify your message.
- Smart nonprofits equip their fans with tools that enable them to spread the word wherever they are online, however they wish. When people use their own voice, they are going to invest more time and will communicate more effectively to their network. Besides, we all know when it is a public service announcement.

- The same goes for organizations distributing content directly. You should always write in a humanizing style, not a robotic or "canned" style.
- Be sure to track your time investment for future resource planning. Remember that participating in social media is an ongoing process and a long-term commitment; just like any relationship, the more time you invest in it, the more you will get out of it.
- Aligning your social media strategy with your organizational goals will help not only change the mindset of your culture but will give your strategy the longest life. You must know your audience and their social technology preference (Twitter, Facebook, LinkedIn®). Each social media application has a different demographic, so target wisely.
- Be pragmatic and realistic in your expectations of your campaign. Your first project will include lots of experimenting and learning. If you shoot too high and miss, some colleagues may want to abort the social media game altogether.
- When getting started, don't be afraid to seek out associates within your organization who are energetic and passionate about social media and get them involved in your campaign. Even if they are not officially in the department responsible for social media, they have experience you can use. They will help ramp up the learning for others and innovate along the way.
- Keep in mind that one of the biggest mistakes you can make is to enlist the help of your social-media savvy colleagues but ignore their input. You need to listen to what they say with an open mind and get behind the great ideas.
- Be sure to set some ground rules for information sharing. Depending on your size, you may want to publish a social media policy manual. The American Red Cross has an excellent example, which has been cited all across the social Web. They encourage staff and chapters to get involved with their social media strategy. It provides various best practices and organizes content in a simple outline.

- Always speak to the constituents' core concerns and forget about being clever. If they care about seniors with low income, speak directly about it. Your constituents are capable, so turn them into fundraisers and give them opportunities to shape the action. Include them in your planning and keep them "in the know." Ask for their input on a program or an event idea.

It's okay to start small. A very simple campaign can have a huge positive impact and gain lots of attention quickly. One of the most successful and inspiring early campaigns (2006), *The Burrito Project*. received the *MySpace Impact Award* for poverty relief. It was started by a single person who rallied a group of friends together to build burritos and take them to the hungry in their community. They launched a MySpace page, published the formula for serving people in the community, and *The Burrito Project* spread around the country and other parts of the world.

Social media has changed the way nonprofits manage their relationships with constituents. Social media–based nurturing tactics have been proven to work extremely well. Encouraging constituents to share their story inspires others to get involved. Pockets of supporters or communities who have been engaged in a bi-directional conversation by the nonprofit are more likely to grow. Keep in touch and keep the relevant discussions going. Together, you can deliver a compelling story that will help increase giving.

A Closer Look at Social Media Tools

Social media covers a large landscape with many different applications, as discussed above. How do you decide which ones to get involved in? Do you try your hand at all of them or select a few? How do I know how many staff members I need to execute my plan? These are all questions that must be answered, but don't let them cripple your momentum in getting started. Remember, learning through trial and error works well with social media; now that it has been around for a while, you can get some great free advice from your tech-savvy peers.

Late last year, several polls were conducted to uncover which channels and tactics people planned to incorporate into their 2009 marketing plans. Social media dominated the results. The most popular were blogging, microblogging (Twitter) and social networks. I would agree that those cover the basic blocking and tackling, but don't forget about other options like the power of a strong video. An engaging story told through a video that links to a landing page where the user can take action (volunteer, donate, fundraise) will likely create a lot of buzz. Video is a much more accessible medium than only a few years ago; it's not difficult to interview family members, donors, or anyone considered a strong advocate and post it online. Keep in mind that most videos can be repurposed, too! It is simple to share videos via e-mail or by embedding them on your Web site or blog.

Speaking of blogs. . . . A blog can be a wealth of relevant information for any organization. It typically is monitored and managed by an individual who posts frequent commentary and tidbits of information on a particular subject. Some are even seen as a form of entertainment. Blogs are often peppered with videos and links to external sites that provide the full details of the topic being reported. The great attribute of blogs is the author's established style and tone and his or her ability to engage the reader to comment into a conversation. The other huge benefit of an active blog is that it will boost your organization's visibility on the search engines with an improved page ranking.

Twitter is the leading microblogging community and is beneficial in several ways. It allows you to receive updates and follow the microblog posts, or Tweets, by leaders in your industry, donor prospects, politicians, community forums, columnists, or anyone else who may provide snippets of news, subjects, rumors, or policies relevant to your organization. I shadow several folks who I refer to as my virtual mentors. Of course, this is a two-way street, so don't hesitate to jump into the discussion and establish a new relationship. These conversations can lead to fruitful opportunities and help your page ranking.

There are hundreds of social networks that your organization can participate in. Some of the most familiar include Facebook,

MySpace®, Ning®, BlackPlanet®, and Eons®. You may hear that you should just be on Facebook, but there may be other networks better suited for your organization. It goes back to who are you targeting, which should drive where you will spend your time. (By the way, the fastest growing Facebook user segment today is the over-55 crowd.) My clients have had great success with Facebook integration. The typical base formula is to create a fan page or group, notify your base to join your "friends" list, and begin publishing interesting and relevant updates about your organization's mission and outcomes. That should be a minimum requirement. Counter to conventional wisdom about social network fundraising, Facebook may be the new frontier for major gifts fundraising. I am referring not to Facebook Causes, which is a remarkable application, but to leveraging third party peer-to-peer fundraising software (such as DonorDrive®) that includes integrated social networking opportunities. In just a short time, this approach has yielded hundreds of thousands of dollars for nonprofits.

Raising Money with Social Media

Fundraising in the social media world can make a big financial splash for nonprofits with inspired ideas like the 12for12k Challenge, which used an outreach strategy and a simple math formula. The challenge is to inspire folks to spread the word about the charity of the month through the various social media outlets each person is connected with. The goal is to get 1,200 people to donate $10 each to raise $12,000 every month in 2009. So far, they have hit their goal each month.

Peer-to-peer fundraising (see Figure 5.1), which relies heavily on personalized e-mail requests to friends and family, is extremely effective. The program begins with an e-mail to your base asking them to register as a virtual fundraiser on your site. Once your constituents complete the registration process, they are able to publish their own fundraising page with a customized appeal. They can easily add video and images to the page that you have provided or that they have created to support your organization. Then the constituent fundraiser imports his or her e-mail address book and sends out a personalized mail to each contact asking for their support. The e-mail includes a link to get involved.

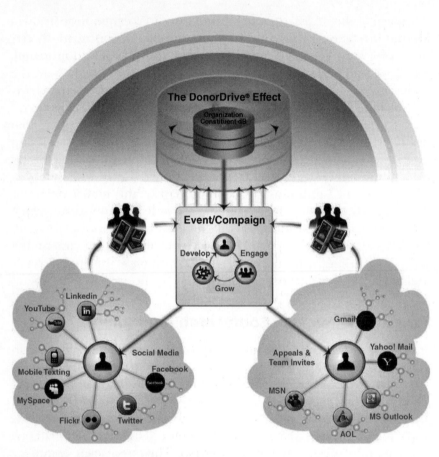

Figure 5.1   The DonorDrive Effect

As new donors join the fundraising cause, the support grows exponentially. The process can be even more effective when that program is coupled with the ability to insert a branded fundraising application on your social network profile page, allowing you to solicit your network of friends for monetary support and connect them directly to your secure donation form. If your organization supports online donations and has established relationships throughout the social media world, you have tremendous potential to drive traffic to give.

Social networking is not the only way to raise money online. Mobile fundraising is a huge opportunity considering there are roughly 250 million wireless subscribers and a rapid adoption of text messaging. The major carriers all accept text donations now, and people are being exposed to mobile giving campaigns more than ever before. The Mobile Giving Foundation (MGF) governs nonprofit mobile giving campaigns. MGF sits between the non-profit charitable giving campaign, the wireless users, and the wireless industry. They help market your campaign, collect funds from the carriers generated by your campaign, and distribute the collections to your organization. Donor contributions are invoiced directly through the donor's phone bill, with the nonprofit recipient specified in order to ensure the tax deductibility of the gift. If integrated properly into your fundraising events and marketing collateral, mobile giving can provide a significant additional revenue stream.

Social Media Impact on Search Marketing

Your Web site should be one of the most cost-effective lures for achieving the results you want. Every organization must carefully plan how to drive more visitor traffic to the Web site in order to communicate the importance of the cause, engage people to volunteer, and increase online monetary contributions as well as provide accessible, current information. (Of course, each nonprofit may have other objectives for Web visitors.) The more eyes and ears land on your Web site, the more people you will build meaningful relationships with.

One very important factor in your ability to successfully drive masses of people to your Web site is page ranking, a term coined by Google to refer to how important a single page is on the Internet. Popularity plays a big role in how well your page ranks. When one page is linked to another page, it is basically endorsing the other page. This attribute is referred to as "link popularity." Additionally, if the page linking to you has a high page rank, then your page appears to be that much more important. Create as many relevant inbound links and you are on your way to winning the popularity contest for your subject. Having lots of social media tentacles linking to you will help. So when a blog, social network page, e-mail, Web site, video, or message board links to your page, you are moving up in the search results.

Link popularity is not the only attribute that can increase your page rank and search engine visibility. Search engine optimization (SEO) tactics will give you an advantage. Content is the number-one SEO attribute and producing current, relevant content will fit well into your social media strategy. Think about it: The search engine's number-one goal is to index and serve up the most accurate and current information based on the user's search keyword or term. As such, the engines know when your site or blog has been updated because they have technology that slurps up your content today and indexes it. In a few days, they do it again and compare the content against the last content scan. If you have been keeping your content fresh, there is a high probability that your site or blog or whatever Web forum will appear higher up the search results page for a given search keyword or term. Of course, there are other SEO factors to consider that influence page rank such as the technical structure of your Web site, title tag composition, domain name handling, file naming conventions, and ADA/Section 508 compliant techniques. I encourage you to study content strategies because it will come in handy when you begin planning out your social media campaigns. Raising your awareness and building your brand will translate into more volunteer, monetary, and partner support.

Major Donors in Social Media

Many big fish—that is, major donors—exist and live in the social media ocean. You just need to find them, right? That is part of it, yes. But what if you thought of major donors as individual influencers who have lots of followers and are daily users of social media tools? Such an influencer might recognize the value in your snippet of content and re-send it out to their network, possibly thousands of people. That one big fish can attract lots of other fish, some of them equally big, to get behind your cause. Before you know it, a wave of donors might flood your bank account, all because of that one big fish. If you add up those donations, they might well equal what you would consider a major gift if it had been one signed check. Instead, through your social media smarts, you have just caught several potential major donors.

A CASE STUDY: AMERICAN FOUNDATION FOR SUICIDE PREVENTION (AFSP)

AFSP's mission is dedicated to understanding and preventing suicide through research, education, and advocacy, and to reaching out to people with mental disorders and those impacted by suicide. In 2008, they conducted 156 fundraising walks in 48 states and rallied over 42,000 participants to raise more than $3.5 million. They created a social media strategy for their community walks to drive participation and giving. The strategy incorporated their Web site and the major social media tools with the goal of empowering as many people as possible on the social Web to promote AFSP by telling their story, recruiting their friends and family, and driving traffic to AFSP's Web site to get involved. Figures 5.2 through 5.10 show a few elements of their social media campaign including a peer-to-peer fundraising Tweet that goes out to all followers each time someone donates, MySpace and Facebook widgets that pull data from and link to personal and team fundraising pages, Team Captain Facebook pages for each market, and increased visibility on search engines because of social media activity and high page rank.

Figure 5.2   Twitter

(Continued)

(*Continued*)

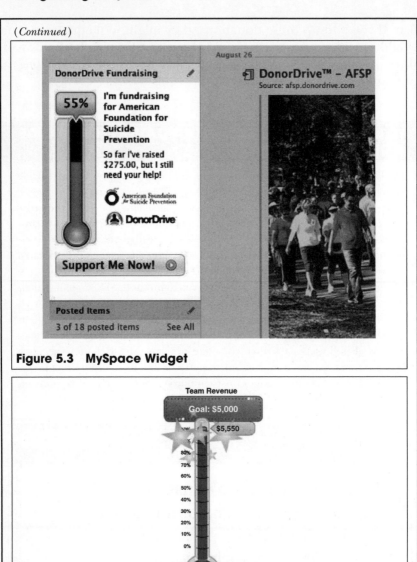

Figure 5.3   MySpace Widget

Figure 5.4   Facebook Widget

Figure 5.5 Social Media Link Box on all Related Sites

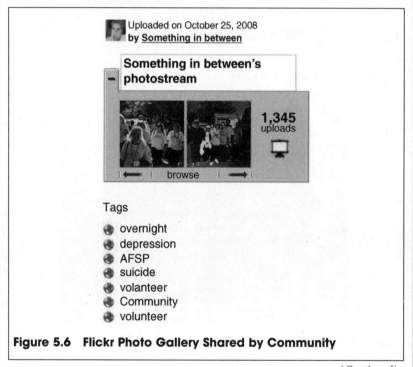

Figure 5.6 Flickr Photo Gallery Shared by Community

(*Continued*)

(*Continued*)

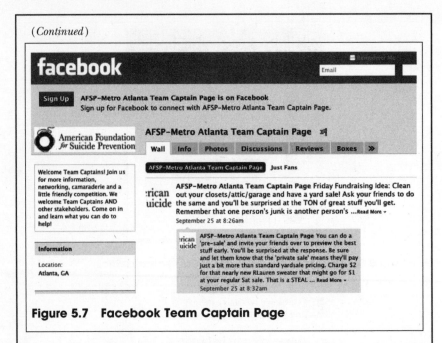

Figure 5.7   Facebook Team Captain Page

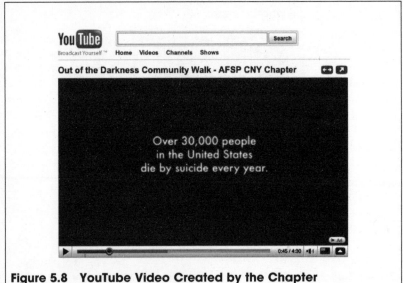

Figure 5.8   YouTube Video Created by the Chapter

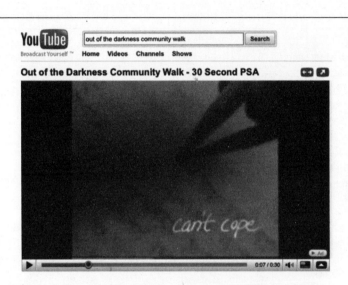

Figure 5.9   YouTube PSA Video Created by HQs

AFSP Community Walks - DonorDrive®
Welcome to the 2009 Out of the Darkness Community Walks! To register for an event near you, click here. To make a donation supporting a participant, ...
afsp.donordrive.com/ - Cached - Similar - ⊙ ⌅ ⊠

AFSP National (afspnational) on Twitter
Preventing suicide through research and education.
twitter.com/**AFSP**national - Cached - Similar - ⊙ ⌅ ⊠

American Foundation for Suicide Prevention (AFsp Suicide ...
MySpace profile for **AFsp** Suicide Prevention. Find friends, share photos, keep in touch with classmates, and meet new people on MySpace.
www.myspace.com/**afsp**national - Cached - Similar - ⊙ ⌅ ⊠

Figure 5.10   Search Engine Example

(Continued)

(Continued)

AFSP Campaign Snapshot

Social Media Initiatives	Metrics	Annual % Change
Blogs	156 walks in 48 states	No change
E-mail Marketing	42,000+ participants	65% increase
Facebook Social Network	3,800+ teams	NA
Flickr Photo Sharing	$3,600,000+ raised	41% increase
Forums/Message Boards	Google Page Rank: 7	No change
MySpace Social Network	Google Links: 592	65% increase
News Feeds	Yahoo Links: 17,900	
Peer-to-Peer Fundraising	MSN Links: 17,500	
Twitter Microblog		
YouTube Video Sharing		

AFSP did an excellent job with feeding content (videos, images, stories) to their constituents who used it to recruit their friends and family. In the end, their message hit every social media outpost possible and they exceeded their goals.

Conclusion

Throughout this chapter, I've covered many areas within the social media ocean. If you have learned a new word or phrase, or if any particular topic has caught your attention, don't stop here! Read more about it online.

As you ponder whether or not to move ahead with social media, remember that driving social change requires embracing new ideas and striking new relationships. Here are the take-aways:

- Social media should be integrated into your organizational goals.
- Learn the basic social media tools first, before planning your first campaign.
- Set your goals, define your strategy, and measure as much as you can.

- Forge relationships with connectors who are influential to lots of people.
- Constantly produce and distribute relevant and valuable content.
- Start small and look long-term at growing your social media footprint.

Social media will allow you to cast the widest net, assist in shaping your organizational culture and build lasting relationships that will be key to your institutional advancement. The conversations you have will lead to answers to your challenges and breathe innovation into your organization to help find a cure, educate our children, service our aging population, preserve our environment, maintain a fair democracy, or support whatever mission motivates you each day.

CHAPTER 6

All Sails Unfurled

Education and Professionalism for Philanthropic Professionals

MARTIN L. NOVOM

Philanthropic professionals often tell me that one of the reasons for pursuing a career in the nonprofit sector has been the great sense of personal fulfillment it brings them. That has certainly been the case for me. Many of us have had discussions with colleagues about the opportunities to earn more money in the for-profit sector. At the same time, one suspects that we might not find the same level of satisfaction that we experience in *knowing* our work makes a difference in the world. While it is certainly true that our idealism is exercised and our social consciousness is stimulated in the nonprofit arena, these have not proven to be the full protection we might like against some common challenges we share with our for-profit colleagues.

Challenges Facing the Career Path Professional

Having had the good fortune to have worked on both sides of the profit and not-for-profit divide, I recognize three shared challenges:

1. Competition and its individual and collective effects.
2. Continuity of employment.
3. Attaining success in one's career.

A great deal has been written in business literature and the popular press about the struggles of professional men and women in this regard. How might these challenges affect us in the nonprofit sector? And what can we individually, and as a profession, do about it?

Competition

Economists, historians, and social commentators describe competition as a key component of commerce and industry. In our market economy, we are told, there is always room for a newer, more cost-effective, or more attractive product or service. All things being equal, it appears that customers gravitate toward the "better" product or service. Competition can be fierce and relentless. Market observers report on the rise and fall of products and the expansion and collapse of industries. Those of us with more than a few notches on our belts have witnessed this.

Alongside the organizational competition, we also have competition for individual jobs. Perhaps like me, you have witnessed the flood of applications for a single job opening. Equally vivid have been my experiences of posting a position and finding no applicants at all. Depending on the circumstances, competition for individual jobs can vary widely.

Depending on the flow of the economic cycle (a rising or falling tide), we may find that there are more or fewer calls for the kind of nonprofit activity we might be pursuing. At the departmental level, individual positions also go through periods of more or less competition. We have seen, for example, an increase in the number of positions being offered for planned giving and for major gift officers.

Employment Continuity

There seems to be a perennial problem of turnover in our field. It means that a large portion of our colleagues are either entering or exiting the field, or as the commonly held notion holds, we are changing jobs far more quickly than best practices might recommend.

Senior professionals tell me that they suspect that continuity in our field suffers under several burdens. It may be that our work attracts more than its share of those with a restless spirit. In my activities as a consultant working across the continent, I see far too many development departments with unrealistic budgets. There are, as well, strong tendencies to hire new philanthropic professionals with insufficient experience, with inadequate organizational support, and often within the context of a poor understanding of the mechanisms of philanthropic programs.

We know all too well the outcomes of these symptoms: quick turnover, voluntary or otherwise, and consequent discontinuities in the fundraising programs. In the training programs where I teach, drawing from the classic 1969 Sidney Pollack film, I tell my students that in our profession: "We shoot development officers, don't we?"

Career Success

The third challenge we share with our for-profit colleagues is that of finding success in one's career. The list of choices we might use to set criteria for "success" is long, highly nuanced, and very personal. However, we might include such items as these (listed alphabetically):

- Accomplishments attained
- Authority accumulated
- Benefits accrued
- Choice of geographic location
- Choice of lifestyle
- Community standing
- Prestige
- Salary
- Savings

I am sure I left out at least one that you might have included.

Beyond factors like these, however, given the mission focus of the nonprofit sector, there is sometimes less separation between personal values and work values than we might expect to find in the work life of our for-profit colleagues. I know CEOs, executive directors, and philanthropic professionals whose life passions mirror the mission of their institution. That isn't to say that sports, recreation, and hobbies are absent from the lives of our nonprofit sector professionals. It is my suggestion that many of us in this field find an outlet for our passion within our work.

Embracing the Challenges

Given that we face these, and other, significant challenges, what can we do as philanthropic professionals to best equip ourselves? Beyond our struggles to meet and overcome shifting economic realities, how do we thrive and grow as individuals? Are we forced, as some voices suggest, to harden ourselves by shedding some degree of our idealism? I certainly hope not.

I believe our ability to grow professionally is dependent on the extent to which we commit to continuous learning. Equally true, it is my conviction that our individual set of gifts will not be fully engaged unless we also focus on the growth of our professionalism.

Many of us place value in attending conferences and workshops, with all the attendant opportunities for learning and networking. When you consider the expansion of social networking and the growth of alternatives to face-to-face meetings, workshops, and conferences, it means we can no longer just rely on the traditional learning methods.

This article has *two major purposes*. First, I intend to discuss how we can incorporate personalized learning into our work and life styles. Secondly, I expect to review how the new and emerging challenges can be best met by an approach to professionalism that reflects the changing landscape of our nonprofit sector.

Lifelong Learning as a Discipline

I have been greatly influenced by the notion that learning is not limited to our years in school. I first became aware of lifelong learning with my introduction to Benjamin Franklin's autobiography and to Booker T. Washington's *Up From Slavery*. It was reinforced with the excitement I felt from my post schooling educational efforts, those that I chose to pursue after I left college and during my career.

I continue to draw great insight and inspiration from the study of biographies of historical figures.[1] When you review the life stories of high-profile, or not-so-high-profile, individuals who have attained fulfilling lives, you repeatedly encounter the practice of lifelong learning. My enthusiasm for biographies is not exactly within the scope of this article, but I do suggest several worthy of your consideration in the endnotes.

What can we learn from these individuals for whom lifelong learning was apparently so valuable? Not everyone who practices a form of lifelong learning has the same philosophy or rationale. I will, therefore, merely try to suggest some commonly stated or exercised practices, particularly those I have come to value.

Learning as a State of Mind

Much of what passes for the education of our country's youth manages to extinguish curiosity. You need only talk to that stalwart group of college professors who work with high school graduates entering higher education. You will hear a litany of stories of a discouraging number of freshmen that have lost the fascination with learning. Assuming that you agree with this observation, what can we do about it? While I might have feelings and thoughts about our national educational practices, I am referring here, of course, to our task as philanthropic professionals.

Learning without joy is a chore. So how do we put the fun back in learning? We can look at an example within our own field, such as when we work to change the perspective of a volunteer solicitor in our capital campaign from one of dread, or the anticipation of a painful encounter, to the experience of joy. My experience in college was like that of a volunteer solicitor who knew he needed to do the work but was not looking forward to it. Now, my approach to learning is quite different. I enjoy it so much that I have to be careful to not let learning take over my life. My desk, briefcase, coffee table, bedside table, bathroom shelf, and the back seat of my car can all get overloaded with books, magazines, articles, and books on CDs (I use them in the car). I expect books on MP3 to make their appearance shortly.

I made the transition from a reluctant, dreading learner to one who embraces new ideas, new concepts and the excitement of fulfilling my curiosity. How did I do this? What happened in my life that brought me to this more energizing place? While I don't assume for a moment that my path fits anyone but me, there might be some kernels of value in it for others.

Despite what I might describe as dismal primary school, lackluster high school, and indifferent college educational experiences, I think the key difference has been my state of mind. It wasn't until long after the bloom of excitement of being in the working world wore off that I discovered that my experience of the world was controlled not by others, but by me. Perhaps this might sound simplistic. All I have is my actual experience to draw upon.

Cultivate a Reading Rhythm

I am thankful that the educational machine did not completely kill my curiosity. Some portion of it survived, revived, and grew into a powerful and life-changing force. Sometime in my middle school years (or junior high, if you prefer), I developed the habit of reading a few minutes every night before going to bed. It is a habit that has grown and taken root in my being. If I go to sleep without having spent at least 5 minutes reading, I feel terribly deprived. Usually it is 30 or 45 minutes. I always travel with books I am reading. Perhaps this is my equivalent of television. What I know, however, is that I have engaged the power of rhythm. Whether it is a novel for the pleasure of reading or a biography of a particular era or type of activity, I continue to learn and expand my knowledge of human beings, relationships and parts and pieces of our world, past and present.

Harness Your Interests

I teach nonprofit professionals in several venues and often use biographies of interesting historical figures to find my way into what might be an otherwise dry subject. It seems most human beings pay attention to stories, especially compelling life stories. Comparing the lives of one or more figures not only makes for lively teaching, but I find it helps me as the teacher to immerse myself in the flow of the stream of a life. My interests are in history and biographies. Are you clear what yours are? More importantly, are you pursuing them? Being able to link your interests to learning is a powerful tool.

Know Your Learning Style

Another area that has become more and more valuable to me over the years has been my growing awareness, and gradual understanding, of how varied the learning process is for different people. The more I engaged in adult education, the more evident it became, that I had to go outside my personal learning style to communicate effectively with others. In my early adult years, I assumed that how I learned was how everyone learned. But as I became a more effective teacher, I realized that if I wanted to be able to "reach" everyone in the class, I needed to utilize different learning styles. Through these experiences I witnessed the range of learning styles of adults.

The purpose of bringing this here is to ask you this question: Are you conversant in your own learning style? Some of us learn best by reading, some by listening, others by writing, still others by clarifying their understanding through asking questions. And, of course, there are many combinations. The more you are able to work with your own learning style, the more your learning is enhanced and the easier you will find it to get the most out of your learning efforts.

The Nexus between Learning and Work

As you no doubt have figured out by now, I see learning as something separate from that which begins and ends with formal schooling. Perhaps this is because my formal schooling seemed so stiff and lacking in creativity.

I approach my work with a kind of learning mentality. Take, for example, my pursuit of a new topic. When I become interested in a new topic, I collect resources on it. In the beginning of my career, when I first understood how important trusteeship and boards were in nonprofit activity, I focused on assembling resources. I quickly went beyond filling a file folder and started a three-ring binder. As the binder became too full, I developed narrower subsets and continued to accumulate articles, citations, and notes. The selection, nomination, and orientation process each became a subset of my interest in trusteeship. You get the picture.

Formal Program Options

There is incredible value in a formal program, be it for a higher degree or for a certificate.

We are fortunate to have seen robust growth in the last decade in formal educational options in nonprofit management, social services management, leadership, and philanthropic programs. Only just a few years ago there were dozens of choices; now there are, according to last count by Seton Hall (www.academic.shu.edu/npo), 294 colleges and universities with programs that focus on degrees for nonprofit management. There are 91 noncredit programs with Fundraising, Managing Your Nonprofit, and Governance as a focus. We have programs at local colleges, state universities, nationally recognized institutions, and prestigious universities.

There are choices for every aspiration size. The first tier, of course, is the certificate programs. These fall in several categories. The most widely known is our certified fundraising executive certificate, CFRE. Now held by more than 4,500 professionals, it is issued by CFRE International to those professional fundraisers who have a minimum of five years on the job, accrue enough fundraising experience, and pass an exam. The next tier is made up of certificate programs available in most states and provinces. Each has a specific focus, be it nonprofit management, fundraising, philanthropy or some other variations. These part time programs are offered by established institutions of higher learning. They are attractive for current professionals and for those considering migration into the nonprofit sector. They vary widely in their depth and focus, but are often attainable with a single course per semester over a couple of years.

The next step up in formal programs is a big one. Assuming that the educational aspirant has a bachelor's degree, the next level of education for our field is a master's degree. It used to be that a master's degree was something you could attain as a full-time student in one or two years. However, very few professionals can afford the luxury of going back to school full time. For those on a career track, especially in management, this is probably a must-have.

The highest levels of formal education, known in academic circles as the terminal degree, are the doctoral level programs. Achieving a Ph.D. in our field is for those who wish to be an educator at an institution of higher learning or perhaps a researcher.

Learning Method Options

The choices of formal educational programs will change from year to year. Changing much more slowly are the methods of learning. This is not your mother's educational landscape. While I just enumerated the levels of formal education, I think it is important to cover some of that same ground to survey the choices in the methods of learning open to career professionals.

In the previous section I described the levels of formal education and made passing reference to full versus part time. These are two of the primary options. Most full-time students are those who are just continuing the educational track from college. Choosing to go back to school full time after having been in the work world to achieve, for example, a master's degree is a life-altering decision. Most professionals do not have the life flexibility to attempt it this way. The most common choice for those already in the stream of career work is to take several years of part-time courses.

In modern life we tend to ignore the pursuit of knowledge outside the formal structure and recognized degrees. It is not entirely fair to say that our culture assumes that the pursuit of knowledge, for its own sake, has little value. I would say that we have become somewhat fixated on the notion that absent the degree we can't leverage learning.

Self-Directed Learning

Many of us don't have a strong enough drive or internal compass to attempt studies on our own. Having done my share of self-directed learning, I know firsthand how difficult it is to stay the course. Even more difficult is knowing how to measure goal attainment or completion. With these words of disclaimer, I want to introduce the values and opportunities for self-directed learning.

Looming large for most of us, when considering further education, is the cost. The price of higher educational programs can be enormous. Taking on a significant debt has become considered a normal consequence of getting a higher degree. Self-directed learning has no such automatic costs. You decide how much expense you can afford or wish to spend. Pursuing formal education has you working to complete a set of pre-determined learning experiences. In our culture we give this experience a name so that others understand the training or experience we have absorbed. We call it a certificate or a degree.

Self-directed learning is for your own knowledge, for your own understanding. It does not have much of an effect on your resume. One could argue that self-directed learning is invisible, or mostly so, to others. Nevertheless, I see that it offers a number of worthy attributes. The low or flexible cost is not, in my opinion, the most powerful benefit.

I believe its strongest virtue is the freedom and the flexibility. I have discovered that self-directed learning offers the opportunity to set your own course. Rather than follow a prescribed sequence, or a predetermined path, you get the freedom to design it yourself. You can set your own pre-determined path or you can leave it open. You have a virtually unlimited set of choices as to both speed and direction. The range of choices need not be limited to what books you read or what writing assignments you take on. Self-directed learning can include, among others things:

- Courses
- Workshops
- Conferences
- Tutors
- Journaling
- Research in libraries
- Access to archives
- Interviews of individuals
- Conducting surveys
- Visits to important sites

What I am describing is, of course, not for everyone. It would be particularly valuable if you chafe under the rigid structure of a formed educational path.

Mutual Learning

While I could include this next option in the general description of self-directed learning, it is worth raising it on its own. I have become aware over time of several versions of what I will call mutual learning. I have seen reading clubs, study groups, and coaching circles. I am sure there are many more variations. Let me describe these.

Reading clubs are at one end of the spectrum. A reading club might describe a group that meets regularly for the purpose of reading a book and then discussing it. These have become quite popular in recent years. My impression is that, depending on the rigor or tone of the group, it could be oriented more toward pure entertainment or toward serious study.

Study groups, as I have experienced them, start with the assumption that the members meet regularly because they want to seriously study a particular topic or range of topics. I know of study groups that have lasted, with shifting membership, for years. They can be centered on a leading personality with experience in the subject matter or they can be facilitated by someone who, like others in the group, has a serious commitment to expanding his or her understanding of the topic. I know of a couple of local AFP chapters that use the study circle format to convene meetings for those who want to study together in preparation for taking the CFRE exam.

A coaching circle is a variation of study groups. Let me offer an example. In a southern U.S. city there is a community foundation that has decided to help development officers who are struggling to integrate planned giving into their organization's philanthropic programs. The community foundation has committed to sponsor an ongoing set of what they are calling coaching circles. These semi-monthly meetings are facilitated by a community foundation staff member with experience as a development officer and highly proficient in planned giving. These are not lectures or presentations but a set of gatherings where an atmosphere of inquiry is fostered. The goal is mutual learning and sharing. The key point in this example is that a subject worthy of study is being approached using a mutual learning design.

These are illustrative of the point I am trying to make. Formal education is structured, measured with timed outcomes. Mutual learning is open to anyone, usually cost free, with far less structure, and tremendous freedom. I see mutual learning as an open horizon.

The Path of Trusteeship—An Overlooked Option

I want to shift our discussion to an entirely different type of learning. Service on a board of trustees is not usually categorized as learning. In our field we tend to discuss trusteeship from the perspective of group performance or group accomplishment. As nonprofit professionals we devote considerable attention to understanding and arranging the education, training, and motivation of the philanthropic proclivities of trustees on our boards. Lots of our attention goes toward aligning board members for individual and collective action in support of our fundraising goals.

I want to look at trustee service from an entirely different perspective. I believe the pursuit of service as a trustee has considerable potential for individual learning, the learning experienced by the individual trustee. I am calling it the path of trusteeship. If you have never served as a trustee, this may seem unusual or even odd. Allow me to explain.

We have in our culture a number of nominal or not so nominal rites of passage. There are many of them and not everyone perceives them as serious transition points in life. A larger list of rights of passage could include such events as:

- Starting school.
- Falling in love for the first time.
- Buying your first car.
- Voting for the first time.
- Graduating college.
- Entering the work world.
- Getting married.

- Becoming a parent.
- Buying your first home.
- Becoming a grandparent.

Each has the potential to be a marker of significance in one's life, a rite of passage. Accepting the mantle of trusteeship can also be a rite of passage. Of course, just as people can move through life more or less oblivious to the potential significance of each major step, well-meaning individuals can choose to become a trustee with little to no notice of its significance in their lives.

I believe service as a trustee has tremendous significance for society. Alexis de Tocqueville, the greatly admired French observer of mid-nineteenth-century U.S. culture, placed great stock in what he called the power of associations. He described in forceful language how we as Americans band together to solve social problems or improve our communities. He was speaking, of course, of our nonprofit organizations. Nonprofit organizations do not exist separately from the steering guidance of the board of trustees (known in some jurisdictions as board of directors).

Being a trustee, in addition to being an important cultural service, is in my opinion, a tremendous opportunity for *individual learning*. Assuming you recognize the value of this notion, the path of trusteeship can be a powerful learning experience. Having served as a trustee, I have witnessed a variety of reasons why people choose to serve. They include:

- A friend they admire asked them.
- The cause is so compelling.
- It allows them to give back to their community.
- The organization changed the life of someone close to them.
- Community service is an important personal value.
- It helps them feel useful and validated.
- It is an expression of who they are.

All of these are true and worthy, and there are many more reasons. What I am most interested in highlighting here is the unique learning opportunity that can accompany service as a trustee.

While many of us have all experienced trustees who seem to either float in place or do what might be identified as the bare minimum, I want us to consider the potential effect on someone who strives to be the best trustee possible. What does it require to be the best trustee one can be? Among other things, it might require:

- Learning the history of the organization.
- Striving to understand the organization's culture or ethos.
- Becoming conversant with organizational financial tools.
- Understanding the concepts and mechanisms of philanthropic programs.
- Becoming familiar with the rules of decision making used by the board.
- Becoming accustomed to a variety of leadership styles.
- Getting to know the senior staff of the organization.
- Learning how the organization fits into the community.
- Determining how the organization compares to others in its nonprofit niche.
- Figuring out how to work with fellow trustees.
- Coming to grips with organizational dynamics.
- Becoming adept at directing growth and improvement of the organization.
- Coming to terms with one's rationale for being on the board.

As you can see, even from this partial list, aspiring to provide high-level service as a trustee can be a challenging and skill-stretching experience. None of what I am saying is, of course, new. What I am directing our attention toward is, however, the opportunity to enter into a zone of learning. If we picture trusteeship not just as service to the organization, but also as a benefit to the trustee, then we are open to the world of learning it represents.

I believe the world of trusteeship is on the cusp of a major shift in the rationale for service. As more and more people recognize the potential for inner growth, I believe that the boardroom will become less a battlefield for egos and more a classroom for learning.

At the same time, I think trustees who float or just get by will be lifted, as all boats are, by the rising tide.

The Pursuit of Professionalism

The second goal of this article is to pose the question, and hopefully to thereby raise the level of our discussion, about the role of professionalism. Nonprofit professionals over the last two decades have witnessed a major shift in public attitudes toward those of us who toil in the nonprofit fields. There are increased expectations, lessened automatic respect, and greater cynicism about our society-centered motivations. The competitive attitude I referred to earlier seems to have infected an alarming portion of our workplace interactions. Civility, it seems, has greatly diminished stature these days.

To help counter this disturbing trend, I want to point us to the importance and redeeming value of increasing our professionalism. The career-minded in our field seem, by and large, to have entered the nonprofit work world in the pursuit of meaning and professional service to the world. Many of us discovered nonprofit activity by accident. In years past, we could note how many of us didn't go to college to enter this work. Great numbers of us went to college and then somehow found our way here. It is fair to say, of course, that some prescient souls perceived early their career intentions and steered their course here all along.

More and more over the past 20 years, and especially now, the ranks of the new and young nonprofit career-minded have come here by a different set of paths. Many continue to shift from the commercial or industrial worlds, seeking greater acceptance of selfless motivation (not for the money). Doing good continues to be a beacon for those who don't find enough personal meaning in for-profit activity. The proliferation of nonprofit degree programs are, of course, peopled by young adults as much as by middle career professionals.

Where once we had considerable numbers who majored in college in English literature, history, the sciences, or the arts and went on to become our nonprofit leaders, now we have a much greater percentage of professionals who came here, more or less, with this zone of the work world in mind. My observation is that the nonprofit ranks are becoming filled, more and more, by professionals.

So, it is my view that if you find professional philanthropic activity as a fulfilling career direction, it is no longer enough to be highly skilled or competent. I think we are witnessing the emergence of a new level, perhaps even a requirement, for a much greater focus on the quality of our conduct. You can have a graduate degree. You can be a certified fundraiser, even an ACFRE. However, if you aren't strengthening the level of your professionalism, I predict that eventually you will find yourself working at a disadvantage, even under a growing burden, that will not be overcome by increasing your skills.

Professionalism Is More Than Proficiency

What do I mean by professionalism? Professionalism is what I describe as the quality of our interpersonal conduct. It is somewhat analogous to what was called, in a previous era, gentlemanly conduct.

BusinessDictionary.com defines professionalism as:

> Meticulous adherence to undeviating courtesy, honesty, and responsibility in one's dealings with customers and associates, plus a level of excellence that goes over and above commercial considerations and legal requirements.

Written in "nonprofit speak," I might write it as:

> Meticulous adherence to undeviating courtesy, honesty, and responsibility in one's dealings with donors, prospects, volunteers, one's colleagues, and the general public. Plus, it is a level of excellence that goes over and above philanthropic interactions, transactions, and legal niceties.

We have become quite adept in our field in ferreting out, adopting, and promulgating the tools, techniques, and general best practices that result in effective and meaningful relationship building. Those are the elements of proficiency. What I am talking about here is our need for best practices in human interactions, in addition to proficiency.

Attaining a Professional Attitude

Assuming, of course, that you are willing to examine my suggestion of advancing professionalism, how does one do so? If it is more than education, more than skill building, how does one develop or foster a greater professional attitude? I believe it starts with the recognition that it is a needed and worthy attribute. If we agree it is important to aspire to, we are still left with the task of making it an essential part of our work persona.

One way to make progress is for us to identify it in the actions of others. I see it rather vividly when observing much-respected, long-time philanthropic professionals. How do they interact with colleagues and constituents that sets them apart? What is it that we observe in their conduct? What stands behind their actions?

I have given some thought to this and have some preliminary ideas, not complete or definitive by any means. We can make progress in advancing our understanding of professionalism if we recognize what might be the necessary underlying conditions. I believe greater professionalism is possible when we:

- Are open to the contribution of others.
- Are confident in our own skills.
- Feel comfortable working in a collaborative environment.
- Have a strong sense of our personal identity.
- Feel we are in alignment with our group and our organizational direction.
- Are able to share the credit for our achievements.
- Value group achievement as much as successful leadership.
- Are aware of our own strengths and challenges.

I am convinced that a few minutes' contemplation will result in your being able to compile your own list of preconditions for professionalism.

Cultivating and Tending Professionalism

If we have a growing appreciation of professionalism and an understanding of some of the necessary preconditions, then we come to the question of inducing it in our work. What does it take to cultivate and foster professionalism for ourselves?

I think about this in terms of what advances or what retards professionalism. I have a somewhat simplistic idea that if I know what builds it and what erodes it, I can make progress by doing all I can to build professionalism. At the same time, I can continue to make professionalism a greater part of my work life by doing all I can to avoid activities that, for me, erode it.

I listed some preconditions previously and, it will come as no surprise, they are ones that apply to me. The more I can foster in myself any of the following, the more I can *build* my professionalism:

- Clarity of my thinking.
- Identification with my purpose.
- Dedication to my goals.
- Employing rhythm in my work.
- Recognizing opportunities in what comes to me.
- Viewing my mistakes as learning opportunities.

So if I know what fosters professionalism and I emphasize those thoughts and activities, what diminishes it? For me this is less clear, but I will attempt to describe them anyway. I find my professionalism *erodes* when:

- My mood rather than my principles dictate my actions.
- I forget it is okay to say "I don't know but I will find out and get back to you."
- I take personally the unthinking behavior of others.
- I strive more for recognition rather than achievement.
- Goal attainment trumps any opportunities to foster the growth of others.

Mentoring Is Not Just for Mentees

I want to discuss two other areas that have a bearing on professionalism. The first of these is the topic of mentoring. It appears that, in our field, we use and appreciate mentoring as a professional development tool, but in my opinion we take less than full advantage of it.

I am familiar with two forms of mentoring, formal and informal. In some chapters of the Association of Fundraising Professionals there are mentoring programs by which younger or newer professionals are paired with more senior members. These are usually for a specific period of time. I have heard that similar formal programs are used in professional organizations in various fields. The second type, more informal, is a loosely formed relationship between a mentee and a mentor. I had such a relationship, tenuous though it might have been. I approached someone I respected and sought their advice. While I did not exercise the arrangement as often as I understand others practice it, it was quite helpful to me.

For both types, formal and informal, the general understanding is that the primary beneficiary is the mentee. I believe that mentoring can be as beneficial for the mentor as for the mentee. It is all in how we set it up and what expectations we have for it. My purpose in discussing it here is that I want to encourage us to consider the underutilized potential of mentoring for mentors.

I participated in a formal mentoring program of my AFP chapter and found it quite beneficial for me as the mentor. My arrangement with the younger professional was a monthly interaction that we chose to conduct on the telephone. For me as the mentor it was an opportunity to:

- Take a break from my daily tasks.
- Explain my work to an interested party.
- Exercise my skills of articulation and explanation.
- Encourage a budding colleague.
- Rethink the rationales behind my activities.
- Experience philanthropic concepts through new eyes.
- Give back to the profession.
- Test my understanding of concepts with an inquiring mind.

While I signed up for the mentoring program thinking of it as volunteer activity, I realized as it was developing that I was benefiting from it as well.

In terms of the topic of advancing professionalism, I believe that being a mentor offers us an opportunity to foster a collaborative attitude and to strengthen our interactive skills. By being a mentor to someone else we can widen our perspective, develop empathy, and increase our positive attitude.

Volunteering for Professionals

The final topic I want to address regarding professionalism is the idea of volunteering as a method of fostering our professionalism. Perhaps no other field of work utilizes volunteers more than philanthropic activities. Our nonprofit organizations incorporate volunteers at practically every level, from the mailroom to the boardroom. As philanthropic professionals, we have considerable experience with volunteers, as solicitors, as committee members, peopling our events, and in our almost continuous efforts to work with our boards on advancing philanthropic behavior and attitudes.

I think that insufficient attention is being paid to the value of volunteering for individual philanthropic professionals. My observation is that professionals who volunteer do so out of some personal interest, as if it was a hobby. It is my opinion that volunteering should be considered a key ingredient in building professionalism, not something done just because you like to do it. Let me be more specific.

Spending regular time striving to be an effective volunteer can:

- Allow us to see volunteering through different eyes.
- Build empathy for volunteers at large.
- Be a great spur to how we think about our own work.
- Cause us to reflect on how volunteers are treated.
- Help us understand the restraints and boundaries of volunteering.
- Give us direct experience of the joys of volunteering.
- Help us see what works and doesn't work for volunteers

Overall, we gain greater fluency and capacity for our interactions with others, be they colleagues, donors, prospects, or members of the public at large. If you are a philanthropic professional, I cannot stress too strongly how important it is to have the experience of serving as a trustee. Until you have served on a board of trustees, you will most likely not understand, at least not to the full depth, what it is that volunteer leaders at that level have to face, have to overcome, and have to go to sleep thinking about.

A Volunteering Strategy

If you agree that volunteering can be a valuable tool in developing greater professionalism, then allow me to urge you to consider pursuing it in an organized and thorough manner. Everyone has their own style for doing things, and I cannot assume what works best for you. Nevertheless, I suggest that taking a proactive, thoughtful approach has considerable merit.

I suggest you consider a volunteer participation strategy by asking questions such as these:

- What do you want to experience?
- What kinds of interactions and at what level will help frame those experiences?
- In what niche do you want to do your volunteering?
- Are you most effective in a proactive stance to volunteering?
- Or do you find your way better by reacting to what comes to you?

If you utilize the same type of thinking and analysis you employ in your work, you will no doubt come up with a workable strategy. You need not rush, but don't take so long that you lose momentum.

Conclusion

In the preceding pages I have offered and explored ways of responding to the changes in our profession. I have suggested that our field is made up of a higher percentage of individuals, than in the past, who are career directed. I make claims that competitive attitudes have reduced the level of civility. Perhaps you agree with me; perhaps you may feel I have overstated my observations. If you find merit in *my* perspective, then I encourage you to consider again, for yourself and for others, the:

Importance of continuous learning.

Need for improving our professionalism.

Value of being a mentor.

Importance of volunteering.

CHAPTER 7

Diversity in Philanthropy: A New Paradigm

JAMES B. TYSON

Diversity in philanthropy, although studied extensively by numerous prominent scholars and practitioners, still remains misunderstood by the majority of the general public. This misunderstanding often extends to those who have chosen to make the so-called "third sector" their life's work. The result is a perpetuation of numerous inaccuracies, misrepresentations, and myths, including one that claims African Americans and other minority groups are not involved in philanthropy because of a lack of financial resources or a lack of commitment to supporting organizations at significant financial levels.

This chapter seeks to present a brief overview of the history and development of black philanthropy; to discuss the disparities in representation among the ranks of professional fundraisers; and to explore specific pathways by which increasing the ranks of fundraisers of diverse backgrounds might decrease these disparities.

The author would like to acknowledge the following individuals: Anthony J. Catanese, Ph.D., FAICP; James L.Fisher, Ph.D.; Sumner Hutcheson III; James V. Koch, Ph.D.; Garvin Maffett, Ed.D; Davis A. Odahowski; Richard A. Smith; Ken Stackpoole, Ph.D.; Charles R. Stephens; and Arto Woodley Jr.

By failing to appreciate the rich history, funding priorities, wealth, and funding potential of diverse populations, organizations have failed to reap the benefits that can be derived by raising their profile among these potential donors. They are choosing to limit the positive benefits that intelligently and strategically cultivating, soliciting, and stewarding these groups would have on their organizations. Furthermore, organizations would do well to create the kind of environment wherein solicitors of diverse backgrounds experience a sense of belonging and support. Natural constituencies aside, what successful business model includes the exclusion of nearly half the population of the United States of America?

This chapter examines the issue of diversity in philanthropy from a different perspective. While most scholarly research has focused on philanthropy among diverse groups from the donors' point of view, this chapter discusses the issue from the perspective of the solicitors.

A Primer on African-American Philanthropy

Prominent scholar and expert on black philanthropy Emmet D. Carson, Ph.D., president and CEO of the Silicon Valley Community Foundation, defines black philanthropy as "the giving of time, talent, goods and dollars, by black people for charitable purposes."

Philanthropy was extraordinarily successful in building the foundation of many organizations that have undergirded the progress enjoyed by African Americans for over 150 years. These so-called "mutual aid societies" took many forms, and were so successful that in 1836, Virginia, Maryland, and other states outlawed their formation. Except for those organized as churches, these societies were denied legal status as a matter of law.

Black churches were, however, the most numerous and among the most effective of these societies. They were among the earliest grantmakers, raising funds to build schools and provide scholarships. "It was philanthropy for and by African Americans that helped establish black colleges and universities," says Rodney Jackson, president and CEO of the National Center on Black Philanthropy.

According to Jackson, the church has played a central role in addressing the immediate needs in the community. As such it has played, and still plays, a vital role in collecting contributions and redistributing charitable funds to address social and community service issues. The black church is the uniting force behind African-American philanthropic efforts, in large part because its congregations provide a continuous source of funding. Because of the indigenous control that African Americans have over the black church and its appeal to different socioeconomic strata within its community, it tends to be at the center of African-American philanthropy.

These churches have been egalitarian environments where personal sacrifice was taught, everyone had the potential to give, and there was an expectation that everyone would give. The process of philanthropy starts with engaging people in the issues they care most about. Rather than viewing African Americans only as recipients or beneficiaries of philanthropy, there is a growing recognition of the combined strength in the community.

The rich tradition of philanthropy that began centuries ago is alive and well in the twenty-first century. One of the key components of historic philanthropy has been the aim of developing models of self-sufficiency. When one considers the rise in affluence among minorities in general and African Americans in particular, the role of targeted, intentional philanthropy designed to create and support a thriving middle (ownership) class has to be seen as a major root cause.

Black Philanthropy Today

George Overholser, founder of the Nonprofit Finance Fund, says, "Fundraising is the black sheep of the nonprofit sector. Charities spend as little as they possibly can on it. By extension, fundraisers are the black sheep of the sector's workforce; second-class citizens to the program staff who are in the trenches every day doing the real work of social change."

Philanthropy is one of the true cornerstones of economic advancement. The African-American community has used philanthropic giving as a survival mechanism, according to Carson; but today, many are directing their philanthropy beyond causes focused on survival into economic empowerment and self-sufficiency.

The total potential for philanthropic giving by African Americans is greatly underestimated. Using data from the U.S. Department of Commerce, Chicago-based research firm Target Market News found that in 2004, African Americans made $11.4 billion in contributions. Of that amount, $7.2 billion went to churches and faith-based organizations and $4.2 billion went to charities, education, politics, and other causes.

Despite perceptions to the contrary, the fact is that African Americans give more than any other group, donating 25 percent more of their discretionary income to charitable causes than whites, according to the *Chronicle of Philanthropy*. On average, black households give $1,614 to their favorite causes. In addition, many black families embrace the practice of tithing—contributing 10 percent of their incomes to the church. And when one considers the rising incomes of African Americans, as reported by the U.S. Census Bureau, the need to see these individuals as potential donors is brought into focus. The Census reports that 5.6 percent of African Americans now earn $50,000 or more annually, and within this group, 20 percent earn more than $94,000.

In his 2007 "State of the Region" report, Old Dominion University President Emeritus James V. Koch discusses philanthropic generosity in Hampton Roads, Virginia. He notes that when controlled for ethnicity, black residents give a significantly higher percentage of discretionary income than any other ethnic group. Blacks gave 8.6 percent of their discretionary income to charity, compared to 6.4 percent for whites, 5.7 percent for Hispanics, and 3.9 percent for Asians. This data is even more remarkable when one considers that blacks have less discretionary income than every other ethnic group except Hispanics.

Black churches themselves have been a significant source of philanthropic support. It is rather disturbing to see that support received from religious organizations, once the cornerstone of support for black education, has diminished over the years. In 2007 and 2008, the United Negro College Fund received only one seven-figure gift from a religious organization. When all gifts from churches are accounted for, there are less than 50 gifts above $5,000 to UNCF in any of the last two fiscal years (see Figure 7.1).

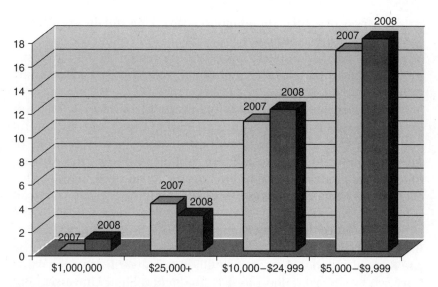

Figure 7.1   Support of UNCF by Black Churches

Source: United Negro College Fund, Inc. Annual Reports.

If that were not troubling enough, there is another potential threat to the historic model of church-based support of community organizations—the emergence of the megachurch.

As seen in the revenues received by the United Negro College Fund, no gift above $5,000 has been received from large non-denominational congregations by the storied organization. From personal observation, whereas traditional denominational churches have supported other community-based organizations, so-called "megachurches" tend to use the gifts they receive from their congregations to perpetuate the church itself.

Mega Trend

The number of megachurches has grown steadily for the last four decades.

Researchers say there are now at least 1,350 such churches nationwide, more than double the number of a decade ago. They draw an average of 4,100 weekend parishioners. By contrast, most U.S. churches attract 500 people or fewer on Sundays.

—Duke Helfand, *Orlando Sentinel,*
October 11, 2009

Since the pool of regular church-goers is shrinking and the growth that these churches are experiencing comes as a result of members leaving other churches, the implications of this movement could have catastrophic consequences for traditional church-based community support.

Beyond giving to religious organizations, individuals of great wealth have diversified their giving. Leading the charge are several well-known individuals. As Carson says, "As a greater number of African Americans become affluent, opportunities for the African-American community to employ more sophisticated methods for channeling philanthropic resources to benefit the African-American community will increase."

Public figures are among the ranks of contemporary African-American philanthropists. High-profile gifts have been made by the late Reginald Lewis, who gave $3 million to Harvard; Attorney Willie Gary, who gave $20 million to his alma mater, Shaw University; Bill and Camille Cosby, who gave $20 million to Spelman College; Wall Street money manager Alphonse Fletcher, Jr., who gave $50 million to endow The Fletcher Foundation; and Oprah Winfrey, who has donated more than $130 million. Others include Tiger Woods, whose Tiger Woods Foundation built a state-of-the-art facility to provide academic support for kids, and Chris "Ludacris" Bridges, who created The Ludacris Foundation to "help . . . youth help themselves."

But clearly not all generous donors are well known. To illustrate the breadth of the donor pool, other not-so-famous philanthropists include the late Osceola McCarty, who bequeathed a portion of her life savings to provide $150,000 in scholarships for minority students. Ms. McCarty was a washerwoman at the University of Southern Mississippi.

Marjorie Polycarpe says, "With greater wealth accumulation among African-Americans, there is an increased need for more sophisticated approaches to direct philanthropy. Today, fundraising professionals and institutional funders are looking at ways to create lasting philanthropic mechanisms within the black community."

The Status of Solicitors of Diverse Backgrounds

For those who have been employed as fundraisers for more than five years and held positions of increasing responsibility, it only makes sense to explore the benefits of becoming a Certified Fund Raising Professional, the professional certification recognized internationally as the credential for fundraisers.

Yet the ranks of professionally certified fundraisers, defined as those holding the Certified Fund Raising Executive (CFRE) credential, remain overwhelmingly populated by Caucasians. Blacks represent 4.1 percent, a 2 percent increase from the previous year, and Asians are the next most represented ethnic group at 2.5 percent. By comparison, African Americans make up 8.8 percent of those in the legal profession, and 3.6 percent of medical doctors.

Ethnicity/Race among Holders of the CFRE

- *88% Caucasian*
- *4.1% Black (2% increase over 2007)*
- *2.5% Asian*
- *1.2% Hispanic (1% increase over 2007)*
- *1.3% Multi-ethnic*
- *0.2% Indigenous persons*

—CFRE Annual Report 2008

Many see the obvious benefits associated with a professional certification. Former President of the Association of Fundraising Professionals (AFP) Charles Stephens says, "The CFRE credential has been proven to be helpful to job-seekers as they pursue their careers. A person of color seeking a position with a nonprofit will significantly increase his or her marketability if they have achieved the CFRE credential."

Others, like President Emeritus of the Council for Advancement and Support of Education (CASE), James L. Fisher, think that a combination of experiences better prepares fundraisers of all ethnicities for successful careers. He sees value in supporting professionals through professional development, including making available the opportunity to attend a CASE Summer Institute or other events. From my own personal experience, I wholeheartedly agree with his assessment. My career is built on the solid foundation I received by attending the Institute at Dartmouth College and bolstered by the credentials I established by becoming a CFRE.

The argument can be made that the impact on fundraisers of diverse backgrounds on their profession and the resultant outcomes mirrors that of underrepresented minority physicians on the health status of that particular segment of the population. In a report by Kingston, Tisnado, and Carlisle,[1] (2001), "Medical training for African Americans first became a topic of policy debate in the United States in the context of the post-Civil War South as a way to address the health needs of the African-American community." It is doubtful that a similar discussion has occurred regarding the presence or absence of African Americans in the fundraising field, at least outside a limited number of institutions, organizations, or associations. To date, the disparity in the field simply has not risen to the level of a sustained national debate.

The trio goes on to say about the status of black physicians, " . . . the best way to meet the great health needs of black communities in the United States was by providing more black physicians." Could a similar thing be said about fundraisers of diverse backgrounds? How much better served would minority, and majority, institutions be if more qualified, trained, experienced, and credentialed fundraisers of diverse backgrounds increased their ranks in the profession?

Sector Analysis

There appears to be a disconnect between the institutions employing the most qualified minority fundraising professionals and the areas supported most by individual philanthropists. Whereas approximately 35 percent of gifts are made in support of religious organizations, this sector only employed 5 percent of all CFREs. The nature of religious giving lends itself to mass appeals by a limited number of solicitors, namely, the clergy.

Education, on the other hand, which received 13 percent of donations, employed 24 percent of all fundraisers. Similar figures can be seen in Health and Human Services (15 percent giving versus 40 percent employment) and the Arts (4 percent versus 7.5 percent employment) (see Figure 7.2).

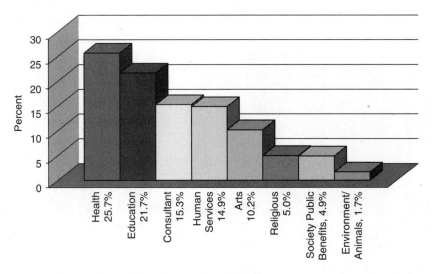

Figure 7.2 Sector of Employing Organization
Source: CFRE Annual Report 2008.

Another way of looking at the data is to say that giving to religious organizations over-performs and giving to all other areas underperforms. The challenge for those seeking support for these underperforming organizations is to close the gap between the level of giving and the relative employment levels of professional fundraisers. The good news is that there is room to realize increased giving to these areas.

According to data from CFRE International, the majority of those holding the CFRE designation are in middle management (see Figure 7.3). As these managers advance into more significant roles in senior management, it is important that they make opportunities available to those who will replace them.

The Changing Role of Women

"It's not just who gives that is changing, but how they are giving and to whom that is redefining contemporary philanthropy." A report conducted by the Foundation Center and Women's Funding Network found that from 2004 to 2006, giving by women's funds grew

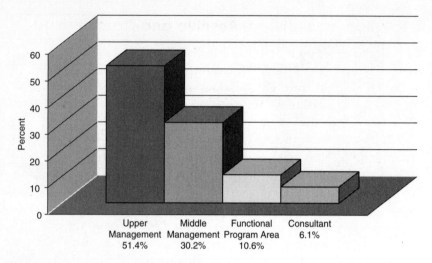

Figure 7.3   Level of Responsibility

Source: CFRE Annual Report 2008.

24 percent, while foundations giving overall grew by 14 percent. These same women's funds saw double-digit fundraising gains during this period; in 2006, they raised $101 million, up from $72 million in 2004.

Women now control more than half of the private wealth in the United States and make 80 percent of all purchases. According to Boston College's Center on Wealth and Philanthropy, women will inherit 70 percent of the $41 trillion in intergenerational wealth transfer expected over the next 40 years. In addition to controlling wealth and consumer activity, women tend to donate more of their wealth than men do—3.5 percent versus 1.8 percent.

CFRE Certificants

- *5,442 Total (new high)*

Gender

- *67% Female*
- *33% Male*

Average Age

- *43 years*

—CFRE Annual
Report 2008

A Solution: Institutional Resolve and Commitment

The call for raising the status of fundraisers of diverse backgrounds comes from many corners. For example, Overholser says, "Fundraising is the front line of civic engagement. Investment in fundraising is investment in understanding social behavior, generosity, altruism, the reasons people give and don't give, why they give, why they give to some causes and not others, and what would make them give more. To understand fundraising is to understand what inspires people and what doesn't. If we want to inspire people to change the world, we would do well to remember this."

As Carson notes, once two of the three arguments used to increase diversity—the "moral imperative," or doing the right thing, and reliance on market forces that dictate that organizations take diversity into consideration in the hiring and promotion processes— are removed, the last argument is merit.

It's not so simple anymore. In Carson's example, a particular organization has three fundraisers: a white male, a white female, and an African American of either sex. Their manager has to assign them to cultivate a particular donor who is a 70-year-old white man. Which one does the manager assign? Suppose the donor grew up in a time when the organization was all white and all male and would welcome seeing someone who reminded him of his days on campus? Suppose the donor has only female children and would love to see someone who reminds him of his daughters? Or, suppose the donor was heavily influenced by black friends and neighbors and was heavily involved in the Civil Rights movement and would love to see an African-American development officer?

The answer ultimately lies in making opportunities available to all fundraisers. Otherwise, personal biases or perceived bias on the part of the donor play out in one officer's receiving opportunities not afforded the others. This leads to the building of a track record of success also not available to the other development officers. This has implications for promotions and over time becomes a self-sustaining and repeating process.

With the increase in the affluence of African Americans and minorities in general, the potential to tap into this under-solicited population also increases. We know that the pool of qualified and experienced fundraisers is thin; the number of those of diverse backgrounds is even thinner.

Richard Smith, vice president for client development at Roosevelt Thomas Consulting and Training in Atlanta, Georgia, has a very good take on how organizations bring about the kind of institutional changes necessary for lasting impact on a diverse workforce:

> Many organizations engage in two primary strategies for diversity. One is focused solely on membership and recruitment. This method is adequate as there is talent everywhere and organizations in this global economy would be remiss if they focused on only one source of talent. What usually comes after this strategy is a focus on workforce relationships.
>
> Now that organizations have brought individuals into the organization who are different, there is usually some tension. This tension is normal and healthy; however, many people have difficulty with its existence. So, organizations will focus on awareness activities, mentoring initiatives to mainstream individuals and other events aimed at building understanding. Considerable effort is placed on these kinds of activities, but what usually happens is that when the organization relaxes these efforts, this diverse talent usually leaves the organization. The question is why.
>
> Since the mid-1980s there has been a growing movement to "bring your full self to work" and not fit a cookie-cutter mold. Leaders can no longer require that an employee behave in a certain way (within reason). Mostly, employees will leave in favor of an environment that allows them to "be themselves."
>
> This leads to the third and, for most organizations, the hardest strategy to execute with regard to diversity, as it requires a focus on culture, systems, leadership style, and on what is really required to get the work done versus what is the preference of leadership, what is convenient for leadership, or a company tradition. This is where the rubber meets the road.

So the question remains: What about fields where there is a lack of underrepresented groups? This is an interesting question, and the answer is: "It depends." It depends on how serious the organization is about getting talent and then managing it in a way that allows employees to bring their full selves to work or, if that is not possible, leaving it up to that individual to determine how much they want to assimilate for the opportunity.

Developing a Pipeline: Looking to the Future

Arto Woodley, president and CEO of Frontline Outreach, sees fundraisers of diverse backgrounds as "underutilized assets." A former fundraiser himself, his perspective also incorporates that of a not-for-profit executive. He thinks that the pipeline is drying up and laments the poor job current and past generations of experienced fundraisers are doing cultivating the pool. Moreover, he thinks "majority institutions seem disinterested in providing opportunities (for fundraisers of diverse backgrounds.)"

Charles Stephens puts it this way: "Fundraisers representing diversity are an endangered species. The numbers are small and getting smaller. Majority institutions are not aggressive about hiring and nurturing fundraisers representing diversity and minority organizations. Because of their size and resources, they are not capable of offering young talented fundraisers the opportunities for professional advancement and cannot offer the competitive salaries available to others in the profession. Non-white fundraisers are, therefore, not opting to make fundraising a lifetime objective."

These sentiments are echoed by Anthony Catanese, president of the Florida Institute of Technology. He thinks that organizations must be committed to creating a cadre of talented fundraisers of all ethnicities. Moreover, he feels that they should not be assigned necessarily to "affinity" fundraising. That is to say, that their skill set should be such that they will be successful working with any set of donors and prospective donors.

Catanese also favors the development of undergraduate programs in nonprofit management and fundraising and notes the oddity of having graduate programs offered without the feeder programs at the undergraduate level.

Stephens thinks, "There is a crying need for academic programs in philanthropy and nonprofit management at colleges and universities that attract people of color and people that represent ethnic diversity. There is not a single program at any university focused on the education of these populations in philanthropic studies or nonprofit management. One or two foundations have funded programs at several majority institutions (Indiana University, Grand Valley University, and the University of Arizona) that were supposedly focused on under-represented populations, but they have not been successful. For me, the operative scenario would be what President Kennedy did when he wanted to put a man on the moon—he engaged the nation's research universities and challenged them to lead the charge. If funding agencies are serious about producing fundraisers and nonprofit managers in underserved populations, programs at the institutions where these students are in the majority should be funded. I strongly suspect that would produce good results. One university leading the way is Claflin University, which has already designed such a program and is seeking funding to launch it."

Sumner Hutcheson, vice president for institutional advancement at Florida Memorial University, concurs with Stephens' Kennedy-era reference. He says, "As in the sixties and seventies, we should get institutions to commit to creating the right environment to assist in the success of fundraisers of diverse backgrounds." Unfortunately, he also relates that he has not seen evidence of that commitment.

Jim Fisher puts it this way: "Ethnicity is not a determinant of success. I've seen good fundraisers of all ethnicities."

Conclusion

Clearly there is a rich tradition of philanthropy by Americans of all ethnicities. It has been demonstrated over many generations that the resources exist to support causes near and dear to the hearts and minds of diverse populations. Also clear is donors' serious intention to support those organizations that serve the needs of the community on the one hand, while at the same time engaging in strategic investment in causes and organizations with a specific expectation of a return. As the country becomes more diverse—it has been widely reported that the population of the United States will become majority non-white in or before the year 2050—it becomes incumbent on leaders to plan for the changes brought on by new expectations and priorities.

For the nonprofit community, there is a significant disparity between the ranks of professional fundraisers of diverse backgrounds and the donors and potential donors who support or could support the nonprofit organizations. When compared with medical and legal professionals—careers which are often reported as being under-represented by diversity—the fundraising profession lags behind. This becomes even more problematic when one considers the future. The gap between current and projected opportunities and the pipeline for professional fundraisers is getting wider. Fundraisers of diverse backgrounds truly are an endangered species.

It will take intentionality of purpose to reverse this disturbing trend. Leaders in several quarters have called for the establishment of formal academic programs, the development of mentoring relationships for both students and those already in the profession, and exposure to networking opportunities. Perhaps Charles Stephens says it best when he says, "The need is huge, not only to assure that existing organizations become sensitive to and serve the special needs of the needful populations in America, but also to assure that community-based organizations are developed and nurtured to maturity to address the escalating issues that threaten to derail all of the ideas that America has historically presented itself as holding and championing. The solutions to the corrosive ills that continue to plague our society emanating from the nation's continually expanding underclass will require the sensitivity of those with first-hand experience *and* formal training. Now is the time to find and train that cadre of professionals."

Appendix A—Black Philanthropy References

Ajayi, J.F.A., and M. Crowder, eds. 1985. *History of West Africa*, 3rd ed. Harlow, England: Longman.

Aluoka, O. 2001. Diaspora Philanthropy: The Promise and Limitations in Strengthening Trans-Atlantic Giving by Africans and African-Americans through Community Foundations. Graduate thesis paper presented to the Center for the Study of Philanthropy, City University of New York.

Atingudui, L. 1995. Defining the Nonprofit Sector: Ghana. *Working Papers of the Johns Hopkins Comparative Nonprofit Sector Project* 14, edited by L.M. Salamon and H.K. Anheier. Baltimore: The Johns Hopkins Institute for Policy Studies.

Aryeetey, E., and H. Hettige, et al. 1996. "Financial Market Fragmentation and Reforms in Sub-Saharan Africa." World Bank Discussion Paper No. 356.

Bohannon, P., and P. Curtin. 1995 [1964]. *Africa and Africans*. New York: Waveland University Press.

Bryce-LaPorte, R.S. 1972. "Black Immigrants: The Experience of Invisibility and Inequality." *Journal of Black Studies* 1:29–56.

Carson, E.D. 1993. *A Hand Up: Black Philanthropy and Self-Help in America.* Washington, DC: Joint Center for Political and Economic Studies.

Carson, E.D., and D. Taylor. 1995. "Black Giving in Minnesota: The Tradition Continues." *Giving Forum:* 1–3. Minneapolis, MN: Minnesota Council on Foundations.

Cohen, A. 1969. *Custom and Politics in Urban Africa: A Study of Hausa Migrants in Yoruba Towns.* Berkeley: University of California Press.

Copeland-Carson, J. 2005. *Promoting Diversity in Contemporary Black Philanthropy.* Indianapolis, IN: Indiana University-Purdue, with Jossey-Bass Publishing.

Copeland-Carson, J. 2004. *Creating Africa in America: Translocal Identity in an Emerging World City.* Philadelphia, PA: University of Pennsylvania Press.

Eades, J. 1980. *The Yoruba Today.* Cambridge: Cambridge University Press, http://lucy.ukc.ac.uk/YorubaT.

Fairfax, J.E. 1995. "Black Philanthropy: Its Heritage and its Future." *New Directions for Philanthropic Fundraising* 8:9–21.

Hamilton, C.V., and L. Huntley et al., eds. 2001. *Beyond Racism: Race and Inequality in Brazil, South Africa and the United States.* Boulder, CO: Lynne Rienner Publishers.

Harris, J.E. 1971. *African Presence in Asia: Consequences of the East African Slave Trade.* Evanston, IL: Northwestern University Press.

Harris, R.L. 1979. "Early Black Benevolent Societies, 1780–1830." *The Massachusetts Review* 20:608–609.

Harrison, F.W. 1995. "The Persistent Power of "Race" in the Cultural and Political Economy of Racism." *Annual Review of Anthropology* 24:47–74.

Holtzman, J., and N. Foner. 1999. *Nuer journeys/Nuer lives: Sudanese refugees in Minnesota.* Boston: Allyn and Bacon.

Iliffe, J. 1995. *Africans: The History of a Continent.* Cambridge: Cambridge University Press.

Jalloh, A., and S.E. Maizlish, eds. 1996. *The African Diaspora.* Arlington: University of Texas.

Joseph, J.A. 1995. *Remaking America: How the Benevolent Traditions of Many Cultures are Transforming our National Life.* San Francisco, CA: Jossey-Bass Publishers.

McDaniel, A. 1995. "The Dynamic Racial Composition of the United States." *Daedalus* 1(124):179–198.

Ogbulie, N. 2001. "Much Ado About Investment Schemes." *Dateline,* October 10, 2001,www.thisdayonline.com/archive/2001/10/15/20011015bus06.html.

Okome, M.O. "African Immigration to the United States: Dimensions of Migration, Immigration, and Exile." A paper presented at Brooklyn College, CUNY, January 16, 2000.

Peel, J.D.Y. 1968. *Aladura: A Religious Movement among the Yoruba.* London: Oxford University Press.

Raji, Y. 1998. "Women in Pre-Colonial Yorubaland, West Africa."*Africa Update* 5(2),www.ccsu.edu/Afstudy/upd5-2.htm.

Siebel, H.D. 2000. "Informal Finance: Origins, Evolutionary Trends and Donor Options. Paper presented at a conference on Advancing Microfinance in Rural West Africa, Bamako, Mali, February 22–25, 2000.

Smith, B., and S. Shue et al., 1994. *Ethnic Philanthropy: Sharing and Giving Money, Goods, and Services in the African-American, Mexican, Chinese, Japanese, Filipino, Korean, Guatemalan, and Salvadoran Communities in the San Francisco Bay Area.* San Francisco, CA: Institute for Nonprofit Organization Management.

Stoller, P. 1996. "Spaces, Places, and Fields: The Politics of West African Trading in New York's Informal Economy." *American Anthropologist* 98 (2):776–788.

Stoller, P. 2001. *Money Has no Smell: The Africanization of New York City.* Chicago: University of Chicago Press.

Walters, R.W. 1993. *Panafricanism in the African Diaspora.* Detroit, MI: Wayne State University Press.

Waters, M.C. 1994. "Ethnic and Racial Identities of Second-Generation Black Immigrants in New York City." *International Migration Review* 28(4):795–821.

Appendix B—Resources

Associated Black Charities

Association of Black Foundation Executives

Association of Corporate Contributions Professionals (ACCP)

Association of Fundraising Professionals (AFP)

CFRE International

Council for Advancement and Support of Education (CASE)

Frontline Outreach

Giving USA Foundation

National Black United Fund

National Center on Black Philanthropy

Nonprofit Finance Fund

Roosevelt Thomas Consulting and Training, Inc.

Thurgood Marshall College Fund

Twenty First Century Foundation

United Negro College Fund

U.S. Bureau of the Census

U.S. Department of Commerce

CHAPTER 8

Twenty Years . . . and Learning

DANIEL YOFFE and
LAURA ZYLSTRA with
DONNA LEIGH KING and
JOHN C. OLBERDING

he bearded gentleman from South Africa stood at the easel and wrote two Chinese symbols. "This," he said, "is how you spell 'crisis' in Chinese. The first symbol is 'danger'; the next is 'opportunity.'"

It was the spring of 1987. Terry Murray was addressing the members of what today is Skystone Ryan. "We face a crisis today in South Africa," he said then, according to those who were there. "The danger is chaos; the opportunity is for transformation."

Philanthropy was vital to the hope of a new South Africa. The tax base in the form of the white aristocracy was in general flight. The policy of apartheid was still in force, though clearly in its last days. There was a trade embargo that would make working in the country difficult. Tribal leaders were jockeying for position in the yet unformed post-apartheid government.

Terry Murray had founded a company that had been active in direct mail fundraising, but he knew that from this day forward something of a different scale would be required.

"We need," he said, "to learn how to raise great funds in a short amount of time."

Thus began our firm's work in the international arena. The first project was to assist one of the country's four "free" universities, the University of Natal (now the University of Kwazulu-Natal), on a 50 million Rand campaign. Since then, the firm has developed consulting partnerships around the world and recruited members who have combined experience working in 34 countries.

And what we have learned over the past decades is that, simply put, fundraising outside the United States is different than fundraising in the United States, for the United States. We have much to teach, to be certain, but also much to learn.

Fundraising is not, after all, an American invention. As early as 2000 B.C., Babylonians were admonished to take care that "justice be done to widows, orphans and the poor." About 1300 B.C., Moses introduced the tithe. And even in recent history, much of what we think of today as fundraising staples in the United States came from overseas. As just one example, the first major walkathons were held in Hong Kong in the 1970s. Indeed, it appears that the impulse toward charity is universal. Every human society has some way of encouraging giving and sharing, though manifested in wildly diverse ways.

With the growth of globalization, more and more nonprofit organizations (NPOs) and non-governmental organizations (NGOs)—terms often used interchangeably, although there are some distinctions—have begun "exporting" their fundraising programs. U.S.-based organizations such as World Vision, JA Worldwide, and United Way Worldwide, for example, now get a quarter or more of their revenue from outside this country. While this trend may seem like a natural evolutionary step for organizations with an international mission, it should not be undertaken lightly. For instance, one of the more common pitfalls for U.S.-based NPOs is to simply believe they can establish and operate the non-Western fundraising offices or practices in the same manner that they raise money from U.S. donors.

Globalization of resources not only expands the potential base of support, but it provides market diversification. Carefully planned and executed, expanding an organization's fundraising frontiers can be a catalyst to growth and a buffer against future economic downturns.

The danger, however, is that this homogenizing approach will result in frustration and wasted resources—not new donors. There are numerous cultural issues and assumptions that U.S.-based organizations ignore at their peril. Both India and China, for example, have long philanthropic traditions, and these two countries' growing economic influences and expanding middle-class populations are attractive to U.S.-based NPOs. But just because a U.S.-based NPO fundraising program is successfully established in India does not mean it can be easily reproduced in China.

Or take language: We must understand that not everyone who speaks a common language speaks with the same voice. Just as we recognize that English speakers around the world speak radically different versions of the same language, we must recognize that accents, words and perceptions change considerably between, for example, Spain and Latin America and within Latin American countries themselves.

Fundraising is intimately connected to the degree of development of civil society and how the idea of philanthropy is installed in it. While in Anglo-Saxon society, government evolved as a consequence of the development and maturity of civil society, colonized nations, particularly in Latin America and Africa, have largely had their societal structures, including philanthropy, imposed.

Moreover, while many U.S. professionals are often driven by our culture's emphasis on "clock time," "due dates," and "return on investment," these same concepts will likely result in the early failures of a homogeneous approach to non-Western fundraising. For reasons such as these, then, the first step of any successful international fundraising effort must begin with country-specific analysis.

With this in mind, we will provide a general overview of important concepts U.S.-based organizations must keep in mind as they consider a worldwide fundraising strategy. We will look closely at a few of the biggest international markets—India, China, and Latin America—examining both the opportunities and the constraints that are particular to each region. Finally, we will consider diaspora giving strategies for engaging first- and second-generation Americans in international philanthropic efforts.

Beginning from the Beginning

When selecting a new market for an international fundraising program, organizations must not only be concerned with generating donors and revenue, but also with creating a quality product, presence, brand, and infrastructure that will effectively support the organization's core mission, as well as enable the long-term retention of new donors. International strategies need sufficient funding, realistic goals, and a flexible time line. Broader organizational and strategic issues need to be addressed before developing and launching a tactical plan. Issues include goal setting and expectations for international fundraising, program deliverables and servicing/renewing donors, development of a strong infrastructure and deliverables, and the process for selecting new markets. It is also important that an organization determine if goals are to be revenue-based, program-based, or activity-based so that expectations for measuring success are realistic.

For instance, large portions of the population of many developing countries, quite understandably, expect their countries to be *beneficiaries* of foreign aid in any of its forms and rarely think of themselves as *donors*. As a result, it is very difficult to raise funds for foreign causes, with the sole exception of natural disasters. This underscores the need to execute local programs, not only because the countries need the services NPOs provide, but also to convey a sense that the organization is contributing to the needs of that country.

Patience is a particular virtue when it comes to expanding a U.S.-based organization's fundraising vista. Expansion into non-U.S. markets is best seen as a long-term investment and commitment. The temptation is great, of course, to merely solicit the most affluent prospects while developing broader relationships and a fundraising infrastructure. This "fly the plane while building it" approach, though, is perhaps even riskier in other cultures than it is in the United States—and it is plenty risky here!

One of the greatest tensions for U.S. nonprofits trying to expand programs, especially membership or fundraising, in a new country involves the amount of time it takes to get a return on investment. The rigid, linear Western concepts of time, coupled with the complexities and difficulties often experienced abroad, can result in frustration and lead to declaring failure and pulling the plug too soon.

It is not uncommon to take at least five years to achieve success in developing a fundraising program that had originally been given an arbitrary goal of three years. For example, a large international environmental organization that started a membership program in Brazil was barely starting to get traction after two years. Some of the early efforts weren't successful, and the staff struggled to adopt and adapt to European/Western tracking and accounting practices. Nevertheless, progress continues, slowly and surely, with a staff person from headquarters making regular trips to Brazil for several weeks at a time to manage the process and continually train local staff.

It is valuable to understand the concept of time from different cultural perspectives. Cultures like those in China and India, for instance, are thousands of years old, so the idea that it could take many years, or even decades, for a business to turn a profit often doesn't faze a Chinese business person. A Western colleague, conversely, coming from a culture whose history is measured in only the hundreds of years, would likely assess successful return on investment in terms of two to three years.

In Latin America, it is taking many years to develop a giving culture, with the single exception of religious giving (which is discussed in more detail later). In some countries, like Mexico, the process is even slower. In this context, large international organizations have an additional responsibility: contributing to the long-term development of a giving culture.

The disparity of perception based on cultural values highlights the need for different ways to view the world when expanding abroad, whether working in a for-profit or nonprofit context. Openness and flexibility is necessary to avoid becoming caught in an ineffective cultural mindset.

This does not mean that an organization should simply accept failure or should commit unending amounts of money to developing these non-traditional donors. Rather, it should plan on being flexible in expectations, anticipating a certain degree of learning "on the job" and applying the advice and experience of other organizations to its own set of organizational circumstances and goals. It should also carefully review the factors necessary for determining the greatest chance for success, both outwardly within the country it wishes to enter, as well as inwardly with its programs and deliverables.

Organizations are encouraged to develop a clear and streamlined process through which countries are assessed and ranked. This is often achieved with the assistance of outside expertise but can be conducted internally if there are staff members with the right background. Unfortunately, the process of determining new markets to enter can be based more on anecdotal information ascertained from professionals inside the country of interest or from board and staff than on careful qualitative and quantitative analysis.

An organization planning to explore international fundraising is well-advised to develop a comparative country analysis process to guide the evaluation, prioritization, and selection of countries under consideration. The analysis process might incorporate several key areas including basic country and market factors, competitors and partners, the organization's in-country presence, and the organization's basic infrastructure at headquarters. The list of factors covered under each area should be developed collaboratively with input from key staff in program, membership, finance, and research, and with the help of outside experts. The factors should include both objective and subjective data, much of which may have already been collected throughout the organization but never consolidated in one place.

The findings will ultimately identify the right countries for the present strategy, serve as a baseline measurement for future analysis, and inform goal setting and tactical planning for moving forward.

We recommend that every country on an organization's strategic horizon be analyzed to inform discussion and decision making for future long- and short-term planning, and to expose any unexpected surprises, opportunities, or challenges. Having this type of data available will help support and explain international strategy and will contribute to stable, long-term planning decisions. In other words, it will answer the "why there?" question. Additional countries, including notes on the rationale, may be added at a later date.

In addition to answering the "why" question, organizations must address the issue of "how to." Tactical planning depends on internal factors, such as program capacity and quality, staff capabilities, and financial resources available for investment, and external factors including laws and regulations affecting nonprofits and fundraising, resources to support fundraising activities, attitudes and understandings regarding philanthropy and competition from other nonprofit organizations.

Many pressing issues impact planning fundraising tactics, including identifying deliverables—what does an organization have to offer potential donors or members in another country? It may not be relevant to simply transfer an organization's U.S. programs, products and services to another country without modification for the local context. Another issue is defining ROI—how should return on investment be defined for a start-up fundraising program? The board, senior leadership, and staff must work together to determine the right mix of financial and non-financial metrics and goals over time in order to accurately set budgets, and measure success and growth.

Fundraising methods that work in the United States can work abroad if the case for support is relevant and tailor-made to appeal to the local market.

A Look at the "Big Two": India and China

Together, India and China have eight times the population of the United States and nearly half of the world's population.

Many U.S.-based organizations are, therefore, understandably eager to expand international fundraising plans to address these two major economies. These are emerging markets, however, and will take much more time and resources to develop than will a program in most European markets.

India

A long history of nonprofit presence and a large English-speaking population makes India particularly attractive to expansion-minded charities. Fundraising has been growing rapidly over the past 10 years due to the rise of the middle class and its increasing profile on the international business stage; the fundraising potential from individual donors is expected to grow significantly over the next 20 years. As a result, India is nearly always one of the markets that international

NGOs (INGOs) consider first when expanding their fundraising. India offers many solid options for growth in nearly any method of fundraising as well as ample challenges. While there are limited resources and no quick or easy answers, investing in fundraising in India holds the potential for paying significant returns on the investment. However, strategies must be developed with one key fact in mind: *by law, money raised in India must be spent in India.* Consequently, organizations should only engage in fundraising in India if there are no plans to export any excess funds raised.

India has a long tradition of charitable giving, though that is overwhelmingly directed to the support of religion. Indian donors also are supportive of humanitarian causes. However, causes addressing the environment and animal welfare are less of a concern in Indian culture, comprising only approximately 2 percent of giving.

> *From the perspective of long-term resource mobilization, Asian and other nonprofit organizations will ultimately depend for their survival on the quality of the relationships they are able to establish with public opinion in their countries and with their own governments, and only secondarily and for the short-term on their relationships with international public and private donor agencies.*
>
> —Barnett F. Baron, Founding Chair, Asia Pacific Philanthropy Consortium

Under Indian law, public charities must be autonomous national organizations with independent governance. Indian NGOs can be set up in three ways: as a society, a public charitable trust, or a private company. Societies, trusts, and companies can apply to exempt the income of the organization from tax under Section 11 of the Income Tax Act. The organization must comply with a range of conditions to be successful and its status is re-assessed annually.

Designing government-sanctioned programs is, based on the number of INGOs in India, achievable and less daunting than it first appears. In fact, many common U.S.-based fundraising techniques have been successfully transferred to India, with direct marketing, payroll giving, monthly committed giving, major donors, special events, corporate sponsorships, and cause marketing all being widespread to varying degrees. Successful fundraising methods in Europe and the United States are typically successful in India when adapted to the local context.

Indians primarily use personal checks to pay bills, make charitable contributions, or purchase merchandise by mail. However, India has seen rapid growth of credit cards, and it is possible to charge a U.S. dollar mail-order purchase legitimately and have this charge processed off-shore. The population of credit card holders is growing at approximately 30 percent to 35 percent a year.

Donations from individuals are the main form of giving to nonprofits in India, and most of the larger fundraising organizations focus on monthly committed giving. Direct response fundraising in India is also used and, to a lesser degree, press, radio, television, and cinema advertising. There are direct marketing agencies throughout India offering a range of support services geared toward commercial clients, but some firms are slowly adapting to service NGOs, including telemarketing and Web design, though quality and cost vary widely.

Multinational companies and national Indian companies have a strong history of charitable support through corporate trust donations and increasingly offer commercial sponsorship, gifts in kind, staff fundraising, volunteering, and so on, usually in exchange for publicity. Local businesses are increasingly available to approach for support, and giving through private family and corporate trusts, at both national and regional levels, is well established in India. The most popular recipients are religious and educational institutions, with health-related organizations third.

A perceived lack of transparency and accountability among NGOs continues to be a problem leading to mistrust from donors. A paper presented by Sampradaan Indian Centre for Philanthropy at the 2002 International Conference for Sustainable Resource Mobilization in Agra candidly discusses the issue:

> Since the 1980s, there has been a rise in NGOs being set up by politicians and fundamentalist religious organizations to skim off funds for political and separatist aims; by private companies as tax

dodges; and by other unscrupulous elements to launder money.
There is also corruption among some government agencies.

Credibility is also linked to location; by and large, attitudes toward rural NGOs are kinder than toward urban NGOs, especially those concentrated in big cities. Rural NGOs are seen to offer help where none exists and have closer interactions with people, so misuse of funds is more easily spotted. Some big urban NGOs have a good reputation; their work is considered essential for society, while many other smaller, lesser-known urban NGOs are suspected of being fly-by-night operators in business for themselves.

Like many other developing countries, India has a shortage of qualified and experienced fundraising professionals. Indian non-profits must work to recruit and retain additional qualified support staff in the fundraising division.

Startup costs for fundraising are affected by the rate of growth desired; the scope of the program; and the budget available for staff recruitment, training and retention. India is not without challenges; but for organizations willing and able to make a significant long-term investment of time and resources, the timing and potential is good.

China

If the philanthropic world needed awakening to the potential of philanthropy in China, that call came from Li Ka-Shing in 2006 as an announcement he would give one-third of his fortune—estimated at over U.S. $30 billion—to charity. He called his foundation his "third son."

Chinese people are accustomed to donating time and money to charity, but not at that level. Li wants his example to begin a new era in Western-style philanthropy. The Chinese culture of "guanxi," or personal connections, means that donations are typically made to groups with which the donor is already familiar. Giving to strangers and unknown organizations has been, to this point, quite uncommon.

Without a doubt, China is one of the most difficult countries in which to conduct fundraising. The government controls every aspect of fundraising, and because the laws are ambiguous, their interpretation can change arbitrarily and without notice. So why are so many nonprofit organizations working so hard to build their capacity to raise funds in China? Because, despite the endless challenges and investment, everyone anticipates that when China pays off, it will be huge; and they all want to be in advantageous positions when the market explodes.

But until that explosion happens, dealing with China's unpredictable government mandates is a constant challenge. For instance, in June 2004, the Chinese government passed a law banning INGOs from fundraising in mainland China. The reason for the law is unclear; speculation ranges from the government's perception that INGOs are "mouthpieces" for Western government to the concern that allowing fundraising from Chinese would result in a subsequent reduction in outside funding coming into China.

Starting a nonprofit organization in China requires the permission of the government at both the federal and provincial level. Once an organization obtains approval, fundraising activities can only be undertaken with permission, which requires a statement of what the funds will be used for and where. The export of funds raised in China also can only be done with the permission of the government. Since Chinese government officials are sensitive to any perception that funds raised in China would be substituted for funds previously received from outside China, proposals for such fundraising are likely to be denied. However, fundraising in China that will supplement or increase the amount of external aid is likely to be approved, due to the interest of the Chinese government for hard-currency funds.

The term "NGO" is used in China to officially refer to two kinds of organizations: social organizations and private non-commercial institutions. In addition, there are Government-Organized NGOs, known as "GONGOs," that are mostly affiliated with state ministries and government agencies. In the past, many of them have been part of (and funded by) a Chinese government agency. Governmental reorganization in recent years has forced these organizations to find their own funding; they obtained NGO status but are still closely related to, and controlled by, their government partners.

While there is no formal regulatory structure for NGOs in China, the government can, at its discretion, impose structures upon NGOs without reference to statutory law or precedent. The legislation for charities has been unclear for a long time and registration is difficult for foreign and local NGOs alike. Most INGOs have a different status and some are not officially registered at all; none of them are entitled to solicit donations in China. An exception is UNICEF, which has approval to do merchandising and direct marketing in China because of its status as quasi-governmental. INGOs are permitted to register as either a National Public Foundation or Non-National Public Foundation; either can grant them permission to conduct limited fundraising activities in mainland China.

China does not have associations devoted specifically to supporting fundraising, but there are a few organizations that support nonprofit organizational development (including general fundraising issues) and direct marketing.

INGOs should give careful consideration before moving into the Chinese fundraising market at this time. While the market is massive and the opportunities are promising, the restrictive government policies regarding NGOs and fundraising make major investment risky at best. Nevertheless, the market is a good one to watch to see when it appears that it might be opening up.

It should be noted that Hong Kong follows British laws regarding fundraising, so it is legal for nonprofit organizations to conduct fundraising activities there that are otherwise illegal on the mainland.

Latin America: A Disparate Region

During the 250 years before the declaration of independence of most countries in Latin America—that is, the first half of the nineteenth century—the Catholic Church was the main player in the field of social services. Charity was the motivation to support projects that were developed to help the poor. The first volunteer organizations in Argentina, Paraguay, and Brazil were the Jesuit missions, which also founded the first schools and universities.

In addition, clergy received donations from members of the community, using them to create educational and health organizations administered by the congregations. Distinguished citizens, guided by their belief in the religious superiority of the rich over the poor, sustained this type of Christian charity, known as "Filantropía Señorial" (gentlemanly philanthropy).

The most important period of development for charitable organizations in Latin America was between independence and the end of the nineteenth century. In 1823 the Charity Society was created in *Argentina*. One of the most notable characteristics of this organization was the involvement of women in the moral education of the lower classes. The participation of women in philanthropic work, which has become one of the most important distinctions of the Third Sector in this country, began as these Catholic charities dedicated themselves to finding homes for the needy, visiting the elderly, and providing food to the hungry. This movement was made possible by donations and monthly subscriptions; additionally, the government frequently offered its assistance through monies raised in the national lottery.

It was during this period that the debate began on the role of public sector financing and its participation in philanthropic and welfare organizations. The increasing number of such organizations toward the end of the nineteenth century was due more to state support and initiative than to any feeling of solidarity or responsibility from the wealthier classes.

In *Brazil*, community participation in social projects began almost with the nation's origin, as the first Holy House of Mercy was founded in San Vicente in 1543. This philanthropic tradition was tied to works inspired by Catholicism, which were a continuation of Portuguese policy since 1498.

It was not until 1938 that the first Ministry of Education and Health was formally established in Brazil, becoming the first government instrument to provide assistance to children and the poor, particularly in the interior of the country. During the 1970s, in a grueling fight in defense of human rights against dictatorship, the Catholic Church exerted its influence with *Liberation Theology*, thereby paving the way for a new (to the region) type of organization, which emerged in 1980: the NPO.[1]

In *Mexico*, the development of the Third Sector and with it, fundraising, was stifled by the Mexican Revolution in the 1920s and the subsequent 75-year dominance of the PRI (Institutional

Revolution Party), which projected the image of a welfare state (although, judging by the poverty levels in the country, it was not).

Nevertheless, throughout the region, NPOs or CSOs (Civil Society Organizations) mushroomed to meet the needs of communities, cities, and countries and filling niches for goods and services that the market is uninterested in providing and government often unable to do so.[2]

In the 1990s, greater business participation evolved throughout the region, and the concept of corporate social responsibility (CSR) has developed considerably in the last 10 years as increasing social disparities have put pressure on businesses to assume new responsibilities. Thus, organizations promoting CSR started emerging in the 1990s, including, among others, in Brazil, Grupo de Institutos, Fundaœões e Empresas (GIFE), and Instituto Ethos de Responsabilidade Social (Ethos); in Argentina, Instituto Argentino de Responsabilidad Social Empresaria (IARSE); in Mexico, El Centro Mexicano para la Filantropía (CEMEFI); in Chile, ProHumana; in Colombia, Centro Colombiano de Responsabilidad Social; and in Peru, Peru 2021.

An indicator of the growth of this sector is the increased emphasis on business philanthropy and social responsibility in major national media, as well as promotional supplements in Argentina and Brazil's major newspapers.

In addition, organizations similar to Independent Sector in the United States, such as the Social Sector Forum(promoted by a coalition of NPOs in Argentina) and the Third Sector Forum in Brazil (promoted by the Serviço Nacional de Aprenziagem Comercial) have been established.[3]

Professionalism, or rather the lack thereof, has been a major setback in the development of the fundraising industry in the region. Nevertheless, professionalism is growing, albeit faster in some countries (Brazil, Argentina, Chile) than others (Mexico, Venezuela, Colombia, Peru, Ecuador, and Central America in general).

An important incentive in local fundraising development in the larger countries has been the decrease of ODA (Overseas Development Aid) as development indicators improved in these countries. Decreasing resources forced NPOs to look for local funding; it therefore became necessary to professionalize the fundraising process.

As a result, academic graduate programs were—and continue to be—implemented in the three largest countries as well as in Chile. The Fundraising School at Indiana University operates in Brazil, Argentina, and Mexico. In the latter country, it is run by Procura, an organization specializing in fundraising professionalism. In Argentina and Brazil, the program attracts students from Peru, Chile, Uruguay, and Paraguay. Hemispheric Fundraising Congresses are taking place in Mexico and Brazil.

Professional associations are seeing the light: the Association of Fundraising Professionals (AFP) has four chapters in Mexico supplemented by The Association of Fundraiser Professionals (AEDROS) in Argentina, the Brazilian Association of Fund-Raising (ABCR), and CEMEFI, the Mexican Center for Philanthropy.

The establishment of major international NPOs/INGOs and the implementation of sophisticated fundraising techniques has also contributed to increase professionalism.

Donation methods are surprisingly advanced. Most countries leapfrogged the check phase and went directly to credit cards, a donation option that became generalized earlier than in the United States. This also eased the way for monthly donations which also became widespread there very quickly, possibly because monthly donations hurt the wallet less than the usually larger single donations.

The legal framework in the region frequently leaves much to be desired as it tends to be bureaucratic, poorly designed, and a barrier to effective resource mobilization. This includes tax incentives for donations, regulatory reporting requirements, and the registration process for CSOs.

In addition, corruption in Latin America has had a negative effect on fundraising. This is clearly unfair, as NPOs have very seldom been involved in fraud accusations; but potential donors nonetheless often think twice before making a donation. Image and reputation for leading organizations are key in offsetting possible doubts when it comes to hitting the "donate" button.

Despite the challenges, there are clear opportunities for U.S.-based organizations seeking collaborations and support in Latin America. As the fundraising field becomes increasingly professionalized in the region, and as U.S. organizations and individuals take an increasingly hemispheric view of many of the issues those organizations address, Brazil, Argentina, Mexico, and other Latin nations are likely to become real partners in a variety of philanthropic initiatives.

Diaspora: New Opportunities and Giving Circles

Increasingly, nonprofit organizations are seeking the expansion of their donor base by reaching out to diaspora populations who will support causes in their country of origin or even among their own ethnic group in their adopted home country.

Discussions of national identity and origin often frustrate common definitions and raise heated debates. In this case, there is an ongoing debate regarding the definition and use of "diaspora" to describe those who live outside their country of origin. We certainly appreciate this debate, but for expedience we will use the word "diaspora" to include expatriates, immigrants, and other non-resident groups, first- and second-generation members from a diaspora family, and anyone else with strong ties to a specific ethnic community.

While there is a growing body of research on diaspora philanthropy, patterns, and trends, there has been limited study of techniques that work for successful fundraising from diaspora communities. One successful technique worth focusing on that has gained particular traction among such groups is the formation and encouragement of giving circles.

Organizations working internationally and seeking to increase diaspora donations often try to establish diaspora connections by communicating their program activities and impact in the diaspora donor's country or community of origin. However, there are often enormous needs within immigrant communities, too. These needs are largely overlooked and underserved by traditional funding channels and, increasingly, diaspora (and first- and second-generation immigrants), are reaching out in response to support organizations that help underserved members of their own communities.

The group Asian Giving Circle describes a giving circle as "a highly participative form of collective philanthropy in which members increase their impact of pooled charitable dollars." Groups of individuals organize themselves to pool financial resources and collectively decide where and how to donate their money. Giving is typically targeted to causes in the city where the giving circle originates.

Giving circles have become increasingly popular throughout the United States within the last 10 years. According to the Giving Circles Network, there are an estimated 800 giving circles in the United States, and they are gaining in prevalence within Asian communities. While the composition of giving circles varies, those in the diaspora communities share some common characteristics:

- Giving circles provide opportunities to network and socialize with others.
- Members educate themselves about issues affecting those in their local ethnic communities and about programs addressing the needs.
- Members pool money, time, and/or in-kind contributions and decide together where and how their money will be allocated— some groups grant funds throughout the year as funds are collected while others build up endowments.
- Asian-American giving circles are composed of a mix of ages and backgrounds, but members tend to be well-educated, young, urban, and professional. Members are often first- or second-generation immigrants.
- Group sizes vary widely, ranging from a few members to over 100.
- Giving circles may choose to organize as a donor-advised fund and have assets managed by a community trust or foundation.

Some nonprofit organizations are approaching giving circles to solicit support. Others are linking with diaspora populations in their service area to organize their own giving circles. For example, the Asian Giving Circle (AGC)[4], based in Chicago, was created in 2002 by three Asian American–serving nonprofit organizations. In addition to contributions made to the three charter organizations, AGC has awarded grants to a wide variety of other organizations serving the more than 30 different Asian ethnic groups in the city.

Giving circle members advise nonprofit organizations to consider the following when approaching or initiating a giving circle:

- The organization's mission and projects should be compatible with the giving circle's interests.
- There must be cultural understanding of the member's ethnic community and its issues.
- Members are busy professionals with limited time so keep engagement simple and meaningful.
- Connecting with diaspora donors takes time and is all about building relationships.

Conclusion

What is the future of international fundraising? A Chinese toast wishes: "May you live in interesting times." These are certainly that. Since Terry Murray met with Skystone Ryan consultants a generation ago to describe a crisis demanding a response from philanthropy, apartheid had finally ended, the Berlin Wall has crumbled, and the Soviet Union is no more. Social and cultural institutions in many countries once supported by the State now look increasingly for vitality and vibrancy to the gentle promise of charity. Meanwhile, the scars of terrorism, two wars, and a devastating recession have contributed to an altered position for the United States in the world of philanthropy. We are, and will likely remain, a leader in that world, but it is incumbent upon us to maintain an awareness of diverse perspectives. We are a more thoughtful nation, perhaps, and one, we would hope, that is more open to the ideas, the values, and the cultures of others. As we seek to advance the mission of philanthropy throughout the world, a thoughtful regard for cultural diversity and local history will enable us to be greeted as valued colleagues by governments, fundraising professionals, and donors alike.

Notes

Chapter 1   A New Day for Philanthropy

1. By way of full disclosure, my son has attended both of the public schools in the county—Clark Montessori and West Side Montessori in Cincinnati—that extend Montessori methodology to the high school level.

Chapter 2   A Person of Influence, A Sculptor of the Universe: How Women Are Changing the Face of Philanthropy

1. These qualifying criteria, as well as much of the following information about giving circles, are drawn from the Forum of Regional Associations of Grantmakers' excellent 2005 publication, *Giving Together: A National Scan of Giving Circles and Shared Giving.*

Chapter 3   The New Nonprofit: How Human Nature, Business Principles, and Financial Realities Are Transforming the Missions, Management, and Finance of Nonprofit Organizations

1. http://www.ashoka.org/social_entrepreneur.

Chapter 4   High-Impact Nonprofit-Corporate Partnerships

1. Polled in a study by The Conference Board regarding the philanthropic plans of major U.S. companies.
2. Carolyn Cavicchio, Senior Research Associate, Global Corporate Citizenship, The Conference Board, The 2009 Corporate Philanthropy Agenda: How the Economic Downturn Is Affecting Corporate Giving, was based on a February

2009 survey of 158 companies on planned changes in corporate giving programs.

3. Anthony Karydakis, *How Long Will the Recession Last?*, Fortune on CNNMoney.com.
4. Charles Moore, Executive Director, Committee Encouraging Corporate Philanthropy.
5. Conference Board June 2009 Corporate Philanthropy Survey.
6. Committee Encouraging Responsive Philanthropy, June 2009 Corporate Philanthropy Survey.
7. Survey conducted by LBG Research Institute.
8. Leslie Pine, senior vice president, The Philanthropic Initiative.
9. Survey conducted by LBG Research Institute.
10. The Foundation Center, July 2009. Figures based on grants and program related investments announced through June 30, 2009. In January 2009, the Foundation Center released a report tracking the initial response of foundations and corporate funders to the economic crisis. This spring, the Center released Foundations Address the Impact of the Economic Crisis based on survey findings that explored how the crisis was affecting funders and their ability to provide support.
11. Committee on Encouraging Corporate Philanthropy, 2008 Corporate Giving Survey.
12. Mary E. Donohue, *The Philanthropy Journal*, September 14, 2009.
13. Stanford Social Innovation Review, Spring 2006.
14. The Conference Board, March 3, 2009.
15. Deloitte 2009 Volunteer Impact Survey.
16. Committee Encouraging Corporate Philanthropy 2009 Summit.
17. Barry Salzberg, CEO, Deloitte LLP, 4/13/09 Press Release.
18. Evan Hochberg, National Community Involvement Leader, Deloitte LLP, 4/13/09 Press Release.
19. Global Trends in Financing the Social Sector, Mirjam Schoning, Schwab Foundation for Social Entrepreneurship.
20. "Outsourcing Back Office Services in Small Nonprofits," A study conducted by the Management Assistance Group in partnership with the Eugene and Agnes E. Meyer Foundation, September 2009.
21. Dan Pallotta, HarvardBusiness.org Daily Alert, September 17, 2009.
22. Aspen Philanthropy Newsletter, September 2009, Aspen Institute.
23. *The Philanthropy Journal*, September 22, 2009.
24. President William J. Clinton; Clinton Global Initiative, Fifth Annual Meeting; New York, New York; September 22–25, 2009.
25. The Committee Encouraging Corporate Philanthropy Web site.
26. The Conference Board Web site, September 28, 2009.
27. The Philanthropic Initiative, Inc. Web site.
28. The Forum of Regional Associations of Grantmakers Web site.
29. Alliance for Effective Social Investing Web site.

Chapter 6 All Sails Unfurled: Education and Professionalism for Philanthropic Professionals

1. I make reference to my study of historical biographies. There are far too many to list here, so I have chosen only those that I feel might be of interest based on the topic of this article: Joan of Arc (*Personal Recollections of Joan of Arc* by Mark Twain was considered by the author his most important book); George Washington Carver (there are several biographies, each with a different slant); Benjamin Franklin (*Benjamin Franklin: An American Life* by Walter Isaacson is a wonderful biography bringing the great man alive and *Autobiography of Benjamin Franklin*); Cabeza de Vaca (*Adventures in the Unknown Interior of America* by Cabeza de Vaca is a little known true story of courage and tenacity by a sixteenth-century soldier in the wilderness); Joseph Merrick (*The Elephant Man: A Study in Human Dignity* by Ashley Montagu is one of several studies of the life of Joseph Merrick, the life of the late nineteenth-century man horrendously deformed but remaining sensitive while overcoming a life of enormous difficulty); Theodore Roosevelt (*The Last Romantic* by H.W. Brands is my favorite biography of Teddy, a larger-than-life character who helped shape our modern world in a number of important ways); Booker T. Washington (the autobiography *Up From Slavery* takes us back to another time, another age, and the struggle of a man transitioning from one way of life to another. The book contains, by the way, a section on how he solicits gifts from wealthy donors.)

Chapter 7 Diversity in Philanthropy: A New Paradigm

1. "The Right Thing to Do, The Smart Thing to Do: Enhancing Diversity in Health Professions—Summary of the Symposium on Diversity in Health Professions in Honor of Herbert W. Nickens, M.D." Raynard Kingston, Diana Tisnado, and David Carlisle. National Academy Press, Washington, D.C.

Chapter 8 Twenty Years . . . and Learning

1. "Fundraising in the Southern Cone." Daniel Yoffe and Renata M. Brunetti. *New Directions for Philanthropic Fundraising.* Number 46, Winter 2004.
2. "How Can Latin American Fundraisers Overcome Current Challenges?" Daniel Yoffe and Brad Henderson.
3. "Fundraising in the Southern Cone," op. cit.
4. To learn more about giving circles, refer to the following resources: The Giving Circles Network (www.givingcircles.org); "Asian American Giving Circles: Building Bridges Between Philanthropy and Our Communities" by Andrew T. Ho of the Council on Foundations; and "The Impact of Giving Together: Giving Circles' Influence on Members' Philanthropic and Civic Behaviors, Knowledge and Attitudes" and "Ten Basic Steps to Starting a Giving Circle," both by the Forum of Regional Associations of Grantmakers.

About the Editors

John C. Olberding

John C. Olberding is president and CEO of Skystone Ryan Inc., one of the leading international fundraising consultancies, with offices in 14 U.S. cities and 11 affiliates around the world. Mr. Olberding's 30-year career in consulting to not-for-profit organizations and non-government organizations includes work as an independent consultant, as a senior consultant with a New England–based firm specializing in health care fundraising. He joined Skystone Ryan in 1986 and has provided a wide range of consulting services, including capital campaign direction, planned giving consulting, and organizational planning to a broad spectrum of institutions ranging from arts and cultural to educational to social service agencies.

Mr. Olberding is past president of the Greater Cincinnati Chapter of the Association of Fundraising Professionals and past co-chair of the chapter's National Philanthropy Day. He is an active volunteer, having served as chapter president of the Evans Scholars Alumni Association, and as a board member of the Catholic Intercity Schools Endowment and St. Ursula Villa. He currently volunteers for North Avondale Montessori.

Prior to his career in development, Mr. Olberding was sports information director at Baldwin-Wallace College and then director of publications for the Cincinnati Reds, where he also served as on-field Master of Ceremonies. He currently is the press box public address announcer for the Cincinnati Bengals.

An alumnus of Miami University in Oxford, Ohio, Mr. Olberding did graduate work at the Athenaeum of Ohio, where he also served as director of development.

Lisa Barnwell Williams

Lisa Barnwell Williams, vice president of Skystone Ryan Inc., has 25 years of executive-level experience in fundraising and organizational development for nonprofit organizations. A superior planner, collaborator, motivator, and implementer, Ms. Williams has served both local and national clients as well as holding senior development positions at Cincinnati Ballet, Cincinnati Playhouse in the Park, Agnes Irwin School, and Whittier College.

With particular expertise in building and nurturing relationships and sustainable organizations, Ms. Williams is a sought-after consultant for board development, constituent relations, and major gifts strategy. She speaks widely on issues relating to nonprofit boards, donor relations, and strategic fundraising.

Before entering the fundraising world, Ms. Williams was a historical documents librarian, with experience including a stint as Project Archivist for the Hubert H. Humphrey Papers at the Minnesota Historical Society.

A past board member of the Cincinnati chapter of AFP, she also has been involved as a volunteer with Children's International Summer Village, Girl Scouts, Business Volunteers for the Arts, and others.

Ms. Williams holds a B.A. from Williams College, an M.A. from New York University, an M.S. from Columbia University, and a Certificate of Advanced Study in Management from the University of Chicago.

About the Authors

Charley Ansbach—During his 30-year career, Charley Ansbach has worked successfully with a wide variety of organizations on local, state, national, and international projects. His key skills are that of strategist and manager who thinks "outside the box," using traditional and new tools to develop workable plans and creative approaches that help organizations reach their management and funding goals. Mr. Ansbach has experience in capital campaigns, public/private partnerships, social entrepreneurism, and venture philanthropy. He regularly assists groups with capital campaigns, organization transformation, board and staff training, pre-campaign feasibility studies, donor interest cultivation campaigns, development audits, and enterprise development. He is an active speaker on current issues impacting fundraising and management. Mr. Ansbach serves on a variety of Boards of Directors and Advisors, including the University of the Pacific's Global Center for Social Enterprise Development, the Positive Coaching Alliance, and the IEM charter school management organization. He received his B.A. from Edinboro University and was a Graduate Fellow in theater design at Indiana University.

Eugenia V. Colón—Over the course of her 20-year career, Eugenia Colón has served a broad spectrum of organizations in the areas of fundraising and communications. Her extensive experience with the higher education community includes particular expertise in corporate major gift fundraising, capital campaigns, and program development. Ms. Colón has managed the completion of the capital campaign for the Clinton Presidential Center and Library and was instrumental in the design, development, naming, and implementation of the historic $1 billion Gates Millennium Scholars Program. She is responsible for obtaining major gifts ranging from $250,000 to $16 million. As a consultant, she has served the William J. Clinton Presidential Foundation, Lawyers' Committee for Civil Rights Under Law, and the Network of Alliances for Bridging Race & Ethnicity. Prior to forming her own consulting firm and then joining Skystone Ryan, she held senior development positions for the Association of Fundraising Professionals (AFP) and The United Negro College Fund. Ms. Colón earned a Bachelor of Arts from the State University of New York, College at Purchase, and a Master's in Public Administration from The George Washington University. She is a Certified Fund Raising Executive (CFRE), a member of the AFP, the E-Philanthropy Foundation, The Resource Alliance, the American Marketing Association, the Association of Proposal Management Professionals, and the Fortune Business Leaders Council. Ms. Colón is an author of numerous articles and a frequently sought-after speaker.

Paul Ghiz—Paul Ghiz has been designing and executing Web strategies for nonprofit organizations since 1997 when he co-founded Global Cloud. His company's mission is to improve lives through nonprofit Web software and services. Mr. Ghiz is a creative entrepreneur and leader with extensive experience in online fund-raising, marketing, accessibility, design, and social media. He has helped architect Web solutions for national not-for-profits and higher education institutions. Mr. Ghiz is a frequent speaker on raising capital and leveraging the Internet, and has contributed to several publications including *Your Career in Advertising*, a college textbook on Web advertising. Before founding his current firm, he was a principal in an Internet broadcasting software company where he led the initial Web strategy for The E.W. Scripps Company. Mr. Ghiz has held Adjunct Faculty positions in Web design and marketing at Miami University in Ohio and currently serves on several boards including the Multimedia Information Design Advisory Board at Cincinnati State Technical and Community College. Mr. Ghiz holds a BFA in Graphic Design from Miami University in Ohio.

Donna Leigh King—Donna King has been securing public and private grant support for organizations in the United States and internationally since 1998. She has worked professionally with some of Greater Cincinnati's leading social service and public health agencies, including Cincinnati Children's Hospital Medical Center, Big Brothers Big Sisters of Greater Cincinnati, The Wellness Community, and The Children's Home of Northern Kentucky. As a former Fulbright Scholar, her international experience includes work with nonprofit agencies in South Africa and China. Ms. King holds a Bachelor's degree from Northern Kentucky University and a Master's degree from Michigan State University. She also studied and taught at the University of Natal in Pietermaritzburg, South Africa.

Martin L. Novom, CFRE—Martin Novom has more than 22 years' experience as a philanthropic professional. His background includes senior executive positions for health care, public broadcasting, and human service organizations. As a recognized expert in the areas of capital campaigns, planning, and leadership development, Mr. Novom has counseled educational, health care, human service, performing arts, and environmental nonprofits throughout the United States and Canada. As one of only 105 AFP Certified Master Teachers, he is a sought-after leader of seminars and workshops and a keynote presenter. Mr. Novom is the co-director of the Administration With Spirit Program, a training program for administrators of Waldorf Schools and other spiritually inspired organizations at Rudolf Steiner College, Fair Oaks, California. He is also the editor and lead author of *The Fundraising Feasibility Study: It's Not About the Money*, a book in the Wiley/AFP Fund Development Series. An active member of the AFP, Mr. Novom serves on national committees and is the past president of the Northern New England chapter. Martin was given the 2009 Outstanding Service to the Chapter Award by AFP of Northern New England. He is a graduate of California State University.

James B. Tyson, CFRE—For more than 18 years, James Tyson has provided fundraising counsel to higher education institutions and social service and civic agencies. His background includes capital campaigns, as well as annual gift and major gifts programs. Mr. Tyson also has extensive experience with external affairs activities, public relations, financial analysis, and strategic planning. Prior to joining the firm, he was vice president of external affairs and served as the chief spokesperson and charitable foundation administrator for the Insurance Office of America. Earlier in his career he held senior development staff positions at the Central Florida YMCA, Devereux Florida Treatment Network, the United Negro College Fund, and the University of Florida. Active professionally in CASE and AFP, Mr. Tyson has also served on various boards, including the Orange County Library, the Metropolitan Orlando Urban League, and the Orlando Regional Chamber of Commerce. He received a bachelor's degree from Morehouse College and did graduate studies in higher education administration at the Old Dominion University.

Daniel Yoffe—Director of Yoffe Castaneda Consultores, Daniel Yoffe is one of the leading experts in fundraising in Latin America, having served as a fundraising staff member and as a consultant to a wide variety of organizations throughout the Americas. His 35-year career in the nonprofit sector began as a Program Officer with the Maccabi Community Center in his native Buenos Aires and evolved into a career focused on fundraising. Mr. Yoffe's experience includes serving as director of the executive training program on resource development at the San Andres University in Buenos Aires. He is guest professor at the Getuilio Vargas Foundation in Brazil and occupied the position of vice president of institutional advancement at the University of the Americas in Puebla, Mexico. He has been a board member of the World Fundraising Council and a professor in postgraduate studies in Nonprofit Organizations at Torcuato Di Tella University in Argentina. In 1997, in cooperation with the Indiana University Center on Philanthropy and the Kellogg Foundation, he opened and was named director of The Fund Raising School for Argentina, Brazil, and Chile. Mr. Yoffe is a sought-after leader in assisting major NGOs throughout Latin America and has published numerous articles for international fundraising conferences and congresses.

Laura Zylstra—Laura Zylstra's fundraising background includes experience in the United States and Asia, incorporating annual fund development, direct marketing, capital campaign management, fundraising program assessment and development, and market-entry planning for international membership and fundraising programs for organizations such as the United Nations High Commissioner for Refugees, WWF (a.k.a. Worldwide Fund for Nature), The Society for Human Resource Management, Habitat for Humanity International, and the Maine Lighthouse Museum. While working in South Asia, based in New Delhi, India, she provided instrumental leadership in the development, implementation, and management of Habitat for Humanity International's ground-breaking Sustainable Funding Initiative throughout South Asia. Ms. Zylstra has designed and led numerous trainings on fundraising throughout Asia and the United States. She is a member of the China Direct Marketing Association (China DMA) and Rotary International. She also serves on the board of directors for the New England Chapter of the Association of Fundraising Professionals.

The Skystone Ryan Prize for Research on Fundraising and Philanthropy

For nearly 20 years, Skystone Ryan has sponsored and funded the Skystone Ryan Prize for Research, awarded annually by the Association of Fundraising Professionals (AFP) Foundation for Philanthropy to the author of a book that contributes substantially to the knowledge and understanding of fundraising or philanthropic behavior. Skystone Ryan's commitment to the Prize for Research is, like *Building Strong Nonprofits*, an expression of the firm's belief that a more comprehensive and multifaceted understanding of philanthropy and fundraising will benefit not only our profession, but our world.

Criteria, Selection, and Honoraria

As the AFP's formal invitation to submit a work for consideration states:

> Authors of published works on research in fundraising and philanthropy are invited to submit books or monographs for the Skystone Ryan Prize for Research on Fundraising and Philanthropy. Other individuals or organizations can nominate appropriate publications.
>
> To be considered for the Prize, works must be:

- A book or monograph of 50 or more pages.
- Published by a commercial publishing house or a professional organization during the 23 months preceding the current deadline (November 1 of each year).

- Based on either applied or basic research.
- Reflect a standard publisher selection process without regard to the source and sponsorship of the research.

The jury will not consider unpublished theses or dissertations, self-published works, directories, op-ed pieces, editorials, or articles.

Prize winners receive a cash award of $3,000 and are honored at the AFP International Conference on Fundraising.

To be considered, a publication must:

- Make a substantive contribution to knowledge and understanding of fundraising and/or philanthropic behavior.
- Have relevance for donors, grantmakers or fundraisers.
- Show creativity and depth of analysis.
- Exhibit quality of style, readability and format.

Previous Research Prize Winners

2009–2010

Global Compassion: Private Voluntary Organizations and U.S. Foreign Policy Since 1939, by Rachel McCleary

Fundraising for international NGOs is a topic of growing interest in the nonprofit world, as individual, foundation, and government funders are increasingly seeing international development as a priority. In this volume, Rachel McCleary considers many aspects of the issue, addressing pros and cons and describing both the present situation and the possibilities for the future.

2008–2009

Money Well Spent: A Strategic Plan for Smart Philanthropy, by Paul Brest and Hal Harvey

Smart strategic planning lays the foundation for smart philanthropy, according to authors Paul Brest, president of The William and Flora Hewlett Foundation, and Hal Harvey, president of ClimateWorks. In *Money Well Spent,* the real experiences of dozens of foundations and other organizations are used to illustrate how to develop and implement a philanthropic strategy that will lead to powerful, mission-appropriate results.

2007–2008

Forces for Good: The Six Practices of High-Impact Nonprofits, by Leslie R. Crutchfield and Heather McLeod Grant

Why do some nonprofits just seem to work? Leslie R. Crutchfield and Heather McLeod Grant search for the answer in *Forces for Good,* a comprehensive, rigorously analytical volume that looks for common principles among a dozen "exemplary" nonprofits, ranging from Habitat for Humanity to Teach for America. The six answers they find provide valuable guidance for nonprofit managers, grantmakers, and policymakers, and also serve to identify some key differences—as well as some important similarities—between nonprofit organizations and their counterparts in the business world.

2006–2007

Contesting Communities: The Transformation of Workplace Charity, by Emily Barman

The meaning of "community" in our era has been the subject of much debate. Charitable giving is both an element of community and its product, and Emily Barman's groundbreaking work provides important new perspectives. *Contesting Communities* uses a careful comparison of workplace charities, including the United Way as well as nontraditional, alternative combined campaigns, to demonstrate the emergence of new models of community. Historical research, survey data, and sociological theory all contribute to Barman's conclusion that meaningful community is a result of purposeful giving.

2005–2006

Uplifting a People: African American Philanthropy and Education, by Marybeth Gasman and Katherine V. Sedgwick

Refuting the notion that philanthropy is the special province of the very wealthy, Marybeth Gasman and Katherine V. Sedgwick examine the depth and power of the tradition of Black philanthropy. *Uplifting a People* considers the history and complexity of African American giving, ranging from the essential self-help among freed slaves with few other resources to the contributions of key figures such as Booker T. Washington and Thurgood Marshall, legal support on behalf of civil rights, diverse contemporary initiatives that encompass education, religion, and the arts. By acknowledging the evolving traditions of giving by African Americans on behalf of their own people, this book changes our expectation, and understanding of philanthropy.

2004–2005

Governance as Leadership: Reframing the Work of Nonprofit Boards, by Richard P. Chait, William P. Ryan, and Barbara E. Taylor

Addressing the necessary division of roles and responsibilities between nonprofit boards and nonprofit management, Richard P. Chait, William P. Ryan, and Barbara E. Taylor help nonprofits reorganize for maximum effectiveness. Drawing on their experience as consultants and on new theories in organizational leadership, the authors not only review traditional board functions in the strategic and financial arenas, but focus on the critical role boards can play in generative thinking. The resulting framework will enable nonprofit boards to move beyond micromanagement into a creative, dynamic leadership role.

2003–2004

Charity, Philanthropy, and Civility in American History, edited by Lawrence J. Friedman and Mark D. McGarvie

Historians Lawrence J. Friedman and Mark D. McGarvie investigate the role of philanthropy in American history and culture by assessing a variety of issues and theories, some of them competing. Ultimately, they conclude that Americans have used charitable behavior to shape the culture, imposing their visions of societal good by forming and supporting like-minded groups.

2002–2003

Opening Doors: Pathways to Diverse Donors, by Diana S. Newman, CFRE

In *Opening Doors*, Diana S. Newman provides an important tool for nonprofit organizations to use in reaching out to nontraditional donors and fine-tuning their messages to a diverse donor base. This book is a down-to-earth guide for fundraising practitioners who want to broaden their funding bases and reach new donors, or improve the diversity of their existing development programs. Sponsored by the prestigious Council on Foundations, the book looks carefully at charitable principles and practices in four broad groups: African Americans, Asian Americans, Latinos, and Native Americans. Employing real-life case studies and examples, Newman provides concrete advice and ideas that nonprofit managers can use every day.

2001–2002

Careers in Fundraising, by Lilya Wagner

In this small volume, Lilya Wagner takes a broad look at professional opportunities in the fundraising field. Preparation, professional development, and job-related concerns are discussed, as is the mission orientation and philosophical commitment required for success in the field. *Careers in Fundraising* is a comprehensive handbook for those considering entering the field, as well as providing expert perspective for midcareer professionals.

2000–2001

Ethical Decision Making in Fund Raising, by Marilyn Fischer
Fundraising professionals face ethical dilemmas every day, and are frequently called on to balance apparently conflicting ethical convictions. In *Ethical Decision Making in Fund Raising,* Marilyn Fischer uses the tools of her field, philosophy, to frame the ethical infrastructure of the fundraising world. Fischer's Ethical Decision-Making Model will enable fundraisers to use their basic values, commitments to their organizations, and personal integrity to develop and support ethical responses to everyday challenges.

1999–2000

Planned Giving: Management, Marketing and Law, by Katelyn Quynn and Ron Jordan
Planned giving can be a foreign country for even the most experienced fundraisers, as it requires comfort and competence in legal, financial, and estate planning arenas. In *Planned Giving: Management, Marketing, and Law,* Katelyn Quynn and Ron Jordan provide a guide that enables fundraising professionals to speak the language, consider the special issues of planned giving, and respect and address the best interests of both the organization and the donor. This core volume is supplemented annually.

1998–1999

Nonprofit Investment Policies: Practical Steps for Growing Charitable Funds, by Robert Fry Jr.
Nonprofit Investment Policies is an essential and accessible guide to nonprofit investment policy for nonfinancial managers. Robert Fry Jr. has written a volume for nonprofit boards and managers alike, illuminating the many issues that must be addressed in managing nonprofit investments in a way that both maintains fiscal health and merits public trust. How to

get started in investments, legal issues, internal management, and public relations are among the issues discussed in depth.

1997–1998

Effective Fund-Raising Management, by Kathleen Kelly
In the first academic textbook on fundraising, Kathleen Kelly integrates social science theory and research with acknowledged best practices to provide a comprehensive view of managing the fundraising function. Legal and ethical issues are explored, as are operational management and the role of fundraising in the organization. Kelly also looks at the historical context of contemporary fundraising practices, recognizing evolutionary developments in both techniques and publics.

1996–1997

Corporate Philanthropy at the Crossroads, by Dwight Burlingame and Dennis Young
During the 1990s, corporate philanthropy began a critical shift in focus, growing from a purely charitable motivation to a comprehensive integration of charitable activity into marketing. *Corporate Philanthropy at the Crossroads,* by Dwight Burlingame and Dennis Young, looks at trends, practices, and underlying issues, providing both insights for the fundraising practitioner seeking corporate support and important direction for further investigation.

1995–1996

The Art of Planned Giving: Understanding Donors and the Culture of Giving, by Douglas White
Planned giving has a very technical side, and practitioners drawn to the legal and financial particulars of the field can overlook its essential human side. These interpersonal and communicative skills are Douglas White's focus in *The Art of Planned Giving.* Drawing on his experience, White provides

both insight into and analysis of the personal dynamics of relationship-building and solicitation. Planned giving officers, fundraising professionals, and board members should read this book before sitting down with a prospect.

1994–1995

Virtuous Giving: Philanthropy, Voluntary Service and Caring, by Mike Martin
Philanthropy is an act of virtue, using giving as an expression of caring for and shaping the future. In *Virtuous Giving*, Mike Martin has written a book for the general reader that explores what philanthropy is all about.

1993–1994

Older Volunteers: A Guide to Research and Practice, by Lucy Rose Fischer and Kay Banister Schaffer
By looking at organizations with exemplary programs for recruiting and working with older volunteers, Lucy Rose Fischer and Kay Banister Schaffer have developed a handbook of best practices. *Older Volunteers* looks at the reasons older people volunteer and considers several models for finding, training, managing, and keeping this key group.

Principles of Professional Fund Raising, by Joseph Mixer
In *Principles of Professional Fund Raising*, Joseph Mixer offers a practical model for building an effective fundraising program and garnering both individual and institutional gifts.

1992–1993

The Commons: New Perspectives on Nonprofit Organizations and Voluntary Action, by Roger A. Lohmann
The nonprofit sector plays a central role in our culture, yet it has received relatively little formal attention, either currently or historically. Roger A. Lohmann takes on the formal study of the sector, defining "the commons" as the voluntary organizations that draw individuals together with common

purpose. Lohmann's integrated vision outlines the common-alities of such organizations, despite vast differences in size, scope, and purpose, including voluntary participation, common purpose, shared resources, and a sense of fair play within the group. *The Commons* develops an important conceptual framework for viewing both contemporary and historical manifestations of the nonprofit sector.

1991–1992

Achieving Excellence in Fund Raising, by Henry Rosso
Henry Rosso, one of the fundraising field's leaders for more than a generation, has contributed a detailed and comprehensive guide to the profession. *Achieving Excellence in Fund Raising* brings together the diverse talents and experience of the faculty of The Fundraising School to provide insights into nearly every area of the nonprofit world. Thoroughly exploring underlying principles, high-level strategies, and practical methodologies, the book presents the issues in the context of cultural practices, organizational values and structures, and donor behaviors. The author includes many practical tools, tips, and ideas to bridge the gap from concept to implementation.

1990–1991

The Law of Fundraising, by Bruce Hopkins
Bruce Hopkins, the acknowledged expert on legal issues pertaining to fundraising, provides a detailed review of the legal environment in which nonprofit organizations operate. Looking at both specific federal and state laws and at trends, *The Law of Fundraising* is detailed, specific, and timely. Cases, rules, regulations, and pronouncements are explored. The volume also includes sample tables and forms. This volume is supplemented annually, and has been reissued in several new editions since the original publication.

Index

Index

Index

Index